Jurors' Stories of Death

MW01036991

Law, Meaning, and Violence

The scope of Law, Meaning, and Violence is defined by the wide-ranging scholarly debates signaled by each of the words in the title. Those debates have taken place among and between lawyers, anthropologists, political theorists, sociologists, and historians, as well as literary and cultural critics. This series is intended to recognize the importance of such ongoing conversations about law, meaning, and violence as well as to encourage and further them.

Series Editors: Martha Minow, Harvard Law School
Elaine Scarry, Harvard University
Austin Sarat, Amherst College

Jurors' Stories
of DEATH

How America's Death Penalty
Invests in Inequality

Benjamin Fleury-Steiner
With a Foreword by David Cole

The University of Michigan Press
Ann Arbor

Copyright © by the University of Michigan 2004
All rights reserved
Published in the United States of America by
The University of Michigan Press
Manufactured in the United States of America
⊚ Printed on acid-free paper

2007   2006   2005   2004   4   3   2   1

No part of this publication may be reproduced,
stored in a retrieval system, or transmitted in any
form or by any means, electronic, mechanical, or
otherwise, without the written permission of the publisher.

*A CIP catalog record for this book is available
from the British Library.*

Library of Congress Cataloging-in-Publication Data

Fleury-Steiner, Benjamin, 1970–
    Jurors' stories of death : how America's death penalty invests in
inequality / Benjamin Fleury-Steiner ; with a foreword by David Cole.
        p.   cm. — (Law, meaning, and violence)
    Includes bibliographical references and index.
    ISBN 0-472-09860-8 (cloth : alk. paper) — ISBN 0-472-06860-1
(pbk. : alk. paper)
        1. Discrimination in capital punishment—United States.
    2. Discrimination in criminal justice administration—United States.
    3. Jury—United States.   I. Title.   II. Series.

HV8699.U5 F54   2004
364.66'0973—dc22   2003017198

For my love and life partner,
Ruth Fleury-Steiner

As an analogy, it was like taking a person, and you play doctor today. We will give you instructions on how to amputate a limb. If we take it off, the patient might regain use of that arm; we do not want you to amputate it prematurely. And now, you decide! We will give you the help of other people, but you cannot ask questions—they will just tell you what they think you should do. I mean, they tried to prepare us, but were we prepared? No, I don't feel like we were. . . . We all looked at each other and said, "Now what do we do?"

—Former capital juror Cynthia Henry

Contents

Contents

Foreword
Shining Light on the Black Box
David Cole

Nothing about the criminal justice system is more mysterious than the workings of the jury. In virtually every other formal legal setting for the resolution of important disputes, we demand an accounting—a written decision, a statement of reasons. Indeed, to a very real extent, the provision of reasons is necessary to law—it is what makes precedent, stare decisis, and the rule of law even possible. Yet the system we have constructed to decide the most important question the legal system ever confronts—whether the state should take a fellow human being's life—relies centrally on a decision for which no reasons must be given.

Furthermore, we have fashioned rules to block inquiry into the jury's decision-making process. The process itself takes place entirely in secret. The jury need only announce a verdict and need not give any explanation of why it reached that verdict. Prosecutors' discretionary decisions also generally need not be explained in court, but as an administrative matter they will often be reflected in the notes taken by the prosecutor. Jurors are rarely if ever even allowed to take notes. And only on extraordinary occasions does the law allow evidence of what went on inside a jury room to be introduced in court; the general rule is that a jury's verdict cannot be impugned by subsequent testimony from the jurors who participated.

What is most extraordinary about Ben Fleury-Steiner's book, then, is that it seeks to shed light on the "black box" of capital jury deliberations. Based on a remarkable social science survey of persons who served on capital juries, this volume illuminates the workings of the most closely guarded secret in the criminal justice system. What he reveals is comforting at one level but deeply troubling at another; in the end, his findings provide further evidence in support of the abolition of the death penalty.

On the positive side, the study illustrates that capital jurors take their jobs very seriously. Whatever else is evident from the many accounts Fleury-Steiner offers, one cannot help but be impressed by the gravity with which all those interviewed appear to have taken their responsibilities. Jurors differed in the extent to which they were pro-prosecution or pro–death penalty and in a host of other presuppositions that they brought to the task, but all these men and women appear to have taken the job extremely seriously. The drama and tension reflected in many of Fleury-Steiner's accounts of confrontations between jury majorities and "holdouts" or "resisters" is precisely a result of the shared understanding of the gravity of the decision they are being asked to make.

But in the end, this positive lesson provides little comfort because Fleury-Steiner's study also demonstrates that no matter how seriously jurors take their job, it cannot possibly be done fairly. Jurors are left to make life-or-death judgments based on partial understandings of the facts and necessarily subjective assessments of personality and life opportunities. And as Fleury-Steiner demonstrates, these assessments cannot help but be colored by jurors' attitudes—conscious or unconscious—about race and class. The fundamental promise and predicate of our justice system is that it is blind to both class and color. The reality, as Fleury-Steiner shows, is that although the black box blinds us to the consideration of race and class, it in no way precludes such considerations. Indeed, because the decisions may be made without stated justifications, biases are all the more likely to play a significant role.

The strength of this book lies in its focus on narrative evidence. Most social science studies of race and the death penalty have been far more quantitative—examining results and seeking through statistics and regression analyses to determine the extent to which racial bias affects outcomes. Fleury-Steiner adds multiple layers of depth and complexity to those studies, virtually all of which have found that race matters. This study seeks to show *how* race matters.

In some instances, the results are predictable. An especially horrific murder by starvation committed by a black defendant leads to the death penalty, but a black female juror and a white male juror arrive at that result along starkly different paths. She is empathetic and understanding and sees the defendant as an individual, albeit one who, in the end, deserves to die for his crime. He, by contrast, dehumanizes the defendant, describing him in racially charged terms as "just like a gorilla. Like Rodney King."

But in other instances, the results are quite surprising. Affinities between the juror and the defendant in race or class terms may make the juror less sympathetic to the defendant. Those who consider themselves closer to the defendant may be less inclined to "excuse" the horrific acts committed by social circumstance because these jurors or people they know may have suffered many of the same circumstances without them leading to murder. Because these jurors feel that they have walked in the defendants' shoes, they feel entitled to judge him for his actions and to dismiss mitigating factors.

At the end of the day, the accounts in this book illustrate that no one can walk in the defendant's shoes. And, therefore, the decision to take or spare a life is inevitably a flawed one, driven by the dynamics of the jury room, personal experiences that are supposed to have no role in the process but cannot be factored out, and skewed rationalizations (for example, the woman who voted to execute a man because she thought that result would be less painful over the long term for the man's mother than having her son alive but in prison for decades, or the person who voted for death while telling herself that "I wasn't the one that was putting the guy to death. The state was.").

We are the state, and we cannot avoid responsibility by pointing to abstractions. This book makes that lesson crystal clear by revealing the intensely human drama involved in declaring who among us will be allowed to remain among the living and who will have his life taken away. Fleury-Steiner's study confirms that jurors assigned this task try very hard and care deeply about what they are doing; at the same time, this book confirms that the task is simply not one that human beings, with all our faults and biases and subjective (mis)understandings, should take on. The job of rendering the judgment to take another person's life ultimately ought never be entrusted to humans.

Prologue
Not "Not Another Book about the Death Penalty"

What more could possibly be said about the death penalty in the United States? Seemingly interminable numbers of scholarly books, editorials, op-ed pieces, screenplays, political speeches, and talk show rants have, for generations, analyzed the topic (no pun intended) to death. The issue recently has again taken center stage. Former Illinois Governor George Ryan's remarkably bold decision to commute all death sentences in his traditionally pro–capital punishment state has intensified the debate anew.

Yet ironically, the questions that animate the current death penalty debate continue to be anything but new: Can the innocent be protected from the death sentence? Is the death penalty racially biased? Is it a deterrent? Does it satisfy the victim family's desire for retribution?

These utilitarian and retributive claims at the center of America's death penalty debate miss one crucial point: Rhetoric is a far cry from the realities of making the decision to impose a death sentence. The failure of contemporary death penalty rhetoric is that it relies too much on abstractions. It is devoid of any measure of the cold, hard reality of having to take the awesome responsibility for another human being's life.

Jurors' Stories of Death is unique in that it explicitly attempts to enter the world of those who do make the awful life-or-death decision: former capital jurors. Hearing the words of those citizens enlisted by the state injects a new and original voice into what has arguably become a debate characterized by boilerplate for or against claims.

In contrast to death penalty rhetoric, *Jurors' Stories of Death* indicts state-sanctioned death sentencing as more than a "broken" legal institution. The interrelated argument advanced here is as follows.

1. By ordering citizens to make life-or-death sentencing decisions, the state invests in cultural understandings that are chained to racist, classist, sexist, and homophobic ideology, beliefs that a vast majority of Americans today would like to see made obsolete.
2. If the United States is striving to embrace the twenty-first-century goals of multiculturalism, including a greater appreciation for cultural diversity, the state's continued use of the death penalty profoundly undermines those goals.

Preface

The social sciences are perhaps better suited for explaining social processes and events than for critiquing or glorifying particular groups or institutions. However, analyses of social phenomena (e.g., punishment) that combine a grounded theoretical approach with the techniques of narrative analysis have advantages over more explicitly quantitative social science research. First, grounded theory focuses the researcher on questions of explanatory import. Second, the techniques of narrative analysis empower respondents to tell their stories in ways that are less encumbered by the categorical rigidity of traditional survey questions. A grounded narrative analysis—obviously contingent on the context under scrutiny—can simultaneously elucidate social processes and expose often unanticipated avenues for robust social critique. In short, hearing the voices of those in power allows researchers to explore social action as it lives in society. At the same time, elucidating the lived doings of power heightens the potential for revealing concrete or tangible perspectives for social change or at least for understanding the processes that inhibit social change as such.

Given its long and contentious history and its highly controversial use today, one state institution that is particularly worthy of scrutiny is capital punishment. Yet the vast majority of death penalty criticism relies disproportionately on either rhetorical claims or the analysis of statistical outcomes as compared to the analysis of the death sentence as it is practiced. That is, the stories of capital jurors' presented here uncover the subtle worlds of "doing death." In this way, I believe the work presented here articulates a more complex and thus compelling critique of state-sanctioned capital punishment than has past research or criticism.

That the death penalty has been at the epicenter of America's protracted struggles with racial inequity does not need to be revisited here—numerous important tomes have well documented this. Rather, the question here is what participating in this institution says about the state of American race relations and our development (or lack thereof) as a multiracial and multicultural democracy. Are we familiar enough with the systems of privilege that characterize our social stations in life to hold the fate of a fellow citizen in our hands? Can members of a society that is still striving to overcome the profound toxicities of race and class segregation and inequity operate a policy as final as the death penalty in a way that even remotely serves America's relatively newfound investments in diversity and multiculturalism?

This book investigates these questions through the lens of one of the most cherished U.S. democratic institutions: the jury. By focusing on the lived experiences of citizens who were enlisted by the state to make the life-or-death decision, this project both invites readers to consider the realities of the death sentence in practice and challenges readers to consider the consequences of its continued use for the future of the American condition.

The approach presented here is thus explicitly multidisciplinary. I certainly could not have written this book without the pathbreaking insights of social scientists such as Jeannine Bell, Patricia Ewick, Jack Katz, Michael Musheno, Laura Beth Nielsen, Trish Oberweis, Cathernie Kohler Riessman, Austin Sarat, and Susan Silbey. I have also been tremendously influenced by critical race scholars such as Derek Bell, Kimberlé Crenshaw, and Patricia Williams; critical whiteness scholars such as Mathew Frye Jacobson, George Lipsitz, and David Roediger; and Lat crit scholars such as Laura Gomez and Margaret Montoya. The imprint of many others too numerous to list is also present in these pages.

While some in the academy have frowned at the obvious breakdown in sociology as a grand approach to social phenomenon, my exposure to the various ". . . and society" and "crit" approaches—with their intensive focus on complex issues such as law, race, sexuality, and gender (social phenomena that are, in my mind, worthy of a disciplinary perspective in their own right) has been truly liberating. Learning about these fields has energized me both as a scholar and as a member of a truly multidisciplinary, intellectual community (in the best sense of that oft overused term).

I would also be remiss if I failed to mention the story of the book's development. *Jurors' Stories of Death* emerges from nearly a decade of work as both a graduate student at Northeastern University and a faculty member in the Department of Sociology and Criminal Justice and the Departments of Black American Studies and Legal Studies at the University of Delaware. This volume grows out of my efforts to understand the pervasive inequities in criminal punishment, especially the death penalty. My doctoral dissertation, "Race, Ideology, and Legal Action" (Steiner 1999), was a statistical study of former capital jurors' beliefs about the legal system in the context of race. While only one drastically revised chapter of the dissertation is included as an appendix here, writing it was an invaluable step in the development of the ideas that fill this book.

More recently, I have collaborated with William J. Bowers and Austin Sarat on a *Law and Society Review* article, "Folk Knowledge as Legal Action: Death Penalty Judgments in a Culture of Mistrust and Punitiveness" (Steiner, Bowers, and Sarat 1999). That work and another article, "The Consciousness of Crime and Punishment: Reflections on Identity Politics and Law-Making in the War on Drugs" (Steiner 2001), which appeared in *Studies in Law, Politics, and Society,* underlie many of my arguments in chapters 2 and 3. Chapters 4 and 5 rely on an article, "Narratives of the Death Sentence—The Tale of Racial Inferiority and African-American Resistance: Toward a Theory of Legal Narrativity" (2002) also published in *Law and Society Review.* Much of appendix B was published as part of "Before or against the Law? Citizens' Legal Beliefs and Experiences as Capital Jurors" (2003).

Between 1996 and 2000, I served as a research associate at Northeastern University's Criminal Justice Research Program. During that period, it was a privilege to be a member of the Capital Jury Project (CJP), a National Science Foundation–funded study of juror discretion in death penalty cases. The data collection effort that yielded the jurors' stories that serve as the focus of this book were supported by this grant (NSF-9013252).

This remarkable and truly interdisciplinary project brought together scholars and students of sociology, political science, criminology, psychology, and law. Without the efforts of my colleagues and their students and without the tireless efforts of countless undergraduate research assistants, the work presented here would never have been possible. I thank the following CJP investigators from around the country for their years of dedication: John Blume (South Carolina), Wanda Foglia (Pennsylvania), William Geimer (Virginia), Joseph Hoffman (Indiana), James Luginbuhl (North Carolina), James Marquart (Texas), Kathryn Russell (Alabama), Marla Sandys (Kentucky), Austin Sarat (Georgia), Jordan Steiker (Texas), Scott Sundby (California), Margaret Vandiver (Tennessee), and Gordon Waldo (Florida). I also thank the following undergraduate research assistants: Laura Biringer, Heather Coutcher, Elisa DiTrolio, Dan Hart, B. J. Hill, Dave Kelly, and Ian Sibble.

Special thanks to my predecessor as research associate, Trish Igo, for her remarkable dedication as the first supervisor and data manager of the CJP, and to my successor, Mike Antonio, for his commitment to CJP 2 (the latest data-collection effort).

I am also grateful for the support of my closest graduate school friends, Patricia Arend and Heather Johnson-McCormick, and to my colleagues at the University of Delaware who read and commented on various versions of this work, especially Margaret Andersen, Ronet Bachmann, Joel Best, Anne Bowler, and Valerie Hans. Moreover, Jeannine Bell, Jennifer Culbert, Jack Katz, Timothy Kaufman-Osborne, Mona Lynch, Anna-Maria Marshall, Sallie Merry, Michael Musheno, Laura Beth Nielsen, Trish Oberweis, Joe Sanders, and Austin Sarat provided invaluable suggestions for improvement. I thank Erin Farley for helping me finish the index.

Phil Pochoda, Jeremy Shine, and Jim Reische at the University of Michigan Press were a pleasure to work with. I also wish to thank Sara Blair for taking the time to share with me some eleventh-hour words of wisdom.

Without my family, I would not have completed this book. I offer loving-kindness to my mother and father, Phyllis and Howard Steiner; my two brothers, Rob and Adam Steiner; Adam's wife, Kerry; and my significant other, Professor Ruth Fleury-Steiner, to whom I dedicate this book. I am incredibly grateful for the love and support of these people.

Finally, I must acknowledge my indebtedness to a great sociologist and mentor, William J. Bowers. My relationship with Bill goes back to the winter of 1994. Soon after beginning as a graduate student in the department of sociology at Northeastern University, Bill invited me to join the CJP, and two years later he hired me as his chief collaborator. His incredible energy for social research created an amazing atmosphere in which to develop my abilities as a sociologist. While we have not always agreed about everything, Bill continually encouraged me to expand my knowledge, to challenge myself to go further in my theoretical thinking, and to ultimately develop my professional identity. I feel privileged to have made his acquaintance and will always be grateful to him.

I do not say that if we understand this man's life we shall solve all our problems, or that when we have all the facts at our disposal we shall automatically know how to act. Life is not that simple. . . . [B]ut whatever we say, let us know upon what ground we are putting our feet, what the consequences are for us and those whom we judge.

—Richard Wright, *Native Son* (1940)

Chapter 1
Introduction

I was crying, driving home from the trial. It caused tension between my husband and myself and my friends. It's like you're in this one bizarre world, and then you go to this other bizarre world, and you can't talk about it. It's awful. I should have never taken that trip.

—Former capital juror Molly Wegler,
describing the day after the jury
made its sentencing decision

I had a part in it. I hate it. I hate that I had a part in it.

—Former capital juror Wanda Nelson,
describing her experiences as a capital juror

Can you imagine? I mean, making a decision to go to a ball game and, you know, losing your life! I mean it's like multiple choice: Should I go to the game, stay home and watch TV, or should I walk my dog? Who would choose to go and be murdered!? I mean, you know, that's something to think about. And I'm not just rambling on, because when I think about it, I'm just—Oh gosh, I can't even put it into words.

—Former capital juror Elizabeth Abbott,
reacting to the murder of two victims who were carjacked
and shot to death on their way to a college football game

Confusion, alienation, anger, and horror: These are the voices of America's death penalty in the latter part of the twentieth century. Far from the high drama of political talk show rhetoric, citizens enlisted by the state[1] to make death penalty decisions, in former capital juror Molly Wegler's[2] words, take a death trip into a "bizarre [legal] world." Leaving their loved ones and everyday lives behind, they are joined by eleven complete strangers. Bringing a myriad of life experiences and perspectives to this strange meeting, they are in effect asked to set themselves aside. Given the law's official orders, citizens as capital jurors are asked to abandon who they are for a theoretical construct imposed on them by the state ("juror"). They are asked to fit a morally complex and emotionally charged decision into a neat and tidy legal category ("life" or "death"). In this book, I argue that who capital jurors are and how they "do death" reveal far more tenuous identities than the state or popular rhetoric would have one believe.

My Approach to the Text

Jurors' Stories of Death represents an attempt to understand one of America's most contentious issues: the continued use of death as state-sanctioned punishment. I approach this issue with obvious apprehension. Indeed, I have hesitated in writing about a topic that I do not pretend to view objectively. Those readers seeking an evenhanded empirical analysis of capital sentencing are thus warned. From the outset, my approach to this study rested on two primary assumptions about death as state-sanctioned punishment.

1. Although America in the post-civil-rights era has made some limited progress in the realm of race relations (Massey 1995; Steinberg 2001), the criminal justice state has largely remained unaffected by such reforms (Tonry 1997). The state continues to target racially and ethnically aggrieved groups, thus exposing them to disproportionately severe punishments, including the death sentence.
2. The web of structural racial inequality that continues to stubbornly characterize much of the American landscape (Massey 1995; Steinberg 2001) has insidious cultural effects. Racial ideologies pervade everyday discourses and thus cultural identities in a myriad of subtle and not so subtle ways.

I believe this exploration will, however, foster new approaches to understanding the complex ways modern state punishment can keep America caught up in its tragically racist past. Hearing the voices of state-enlisted laypersons provides a sophisticated critique of the complex political, cultural, and institutional processes that reveal the pervasiveness of inequities in the American criminal justice system as a whole and in the death penalty in particular.

Jurors' stories set this book apart from previous studies of punishment and the death penalty. In contrast to studies that test a set of theoretical assumptions based on the sentencing outcome, I worked in a more reflexive manner that incorporated theory and insights from the data. While I do not and cannot seek to investigate questions of causality in sentencing outcomes, I believe this analysis presents a complex picture of death penalty judgments that was possible to see only by privileging jurors' stories. Working inductively with jurors' stories, this analysis provides a fascinating complement to prior quantitative analyses of the death penalty (e.g., Baldus, Woodworth, and Pulaski 1990).

Jurors' decisions do not occur in a stable, formally legalistic world. Hearing their stories reveals how the disproportionate sentencing of poor whites and marginalized racial and ethnic minorities is not separate from the culturally embedded and polarizing narratives heard variously throughout American history (Lott 1999). Nevertheless, this us-and-them story of American society and the criminal justice system in particular needs theoretical clarification. As I will argue, it is typically not the obvious and stable articulation of *us* and *them* (e.g., blacks are an inferior, inherently criminal race) that helps to explain persistent inequities in the contemporary American criminal justice system, including death penalty judgments: the instability of identities reveals the stubborn persistence of such inequities.

Identities and Punishment

The routines of social intercourse in established settings allow us to deal with anticipated others without special attention or thought.

> When a stranger comes into our presence, then, first appearances are
> likely to enable us to anticipate his category and attributes, his
> "social identity"—to use a term that is better than "social status"
> because personal attributes such as "honesty" are involved, as well
> as structural ones, like "occupation."
>   We lean on these anticipations that we have, transforming them
> into normative expectations, into righteously presented demands.
>
> —Erving Goffman, *Stigma:*
> *Notes on the Management of Spoiled Identity* (1963)

Inequity in punishment practices is obscured in the multiple and
often overlapping identities of the punisher and the punished. Who
capital jurors are has implications for understanding how they see
defendants and victims and for what punishment jurors will impose.
As the great sociologist Erving Goffman observed nearly four
decades ago, the who, or social identity, of an individual actor is
understood simultaneously at the personal, biographical, and structural levels. Whiteness has historically been represented as safe, law-
abiding, and moral, in contrast to blackness. In this way, the contemporary criminal justice system's well-documented differential
treatment of poor blacks cannot typically be understood as the result
of overt discrimination, as in other historical periods,[3] but rather as
the function of the dominant group's normative expectations of
poor blacks as dangerous, lawless, or immoral. "As righteously presented demands" (Goffman 1963, 137), the modern rage to punish
marginalized individuals is realized in the normative grammars of a
privileged, moral majority. In this way, difference is taken for
granted in dominant discourses on criminals and race more broadly:

> Race conventions can seem to be natural and quite consistent
> with reason, and because they convey significant social mean-
> ings, people with particular race-markers may become stig-
> matized—seen by their fellows as "damaged goods," as
> THEM not US, as persons who lack the ability or "culture" to
> succeed in society's mainstream. (Loury 2002, 111)

Seeing marginalized individuals as damaged goods is not an
abstract process of identification; stories of *us* and *them* are real-

ized in contemporary discourses of success and failure, right and wrong, moral and immoral.

The Normative Grammars of Punishment

> The psychiatrist talked about methamphetamines and that they can make you not aware of your doings and such. I thought it was a crock. I used them when I was in college. When they asked me during jury selection if I had ever used drugs, I said, "Yeah, I have." So when I was listening to this drug expert, I was thinking, "Have you ever done this stuff? Do you actually know what it does, or is this all just textbook knowledge?" He knew nothing, [but I did know,] because I had done this stuff. . . . I shared this with the other jurors, because there was another girl who was also a former addict and an alcoholic. She was hysterical during deliberations and told the jury, "I've done this stuff, used it, done it, and I wouldn't say 'Let's go kill somebody today and get cash for drugs.' " I never was up for four or five or six days as he apparently was. Even so, when you do drugs, you know its illegal, you know it's wrong. So I just believe you're responsible for your own actions.
>
> —Former capital juror Madeline Kraft,
> explaining her reaction to a defense psychiatrist's testimony
> regarding defendant Stephen Ralphs's
> addiction to crystal methamphetamine

> There is also in reality a "normative" grammar . . . a grammatical conformism, to establish "norms" or judgments of correctness or incorrectness. But this "spontaneous" expression of grammatical conformity is necessarily disconnected. . . . If one starts from the assumption of centralizing what already exists in a diffused, scattered but inorganic and incoherent state, it seems obvious that an opposition on principle is not rational.
>
> —Antonio Gramsci, "How Many Forms
> of Grammar Can There Be?" (1925)

Jurors such as Madeline Kraft combine multiple identities—former drug user and law-abiding citizen as juror—to make sense of the defendant's "criminal" identity. As an "everybody is responsible for his or her own actions" story,[4] Madeline Kraft's tale does not have to assess who the defendant, Stephen Ralphs, is. The incoherence of her story enables her to leap from "my life" to "his life" without actually evaluating Stephen Ralphs's life. But who she is enables her to not have to know the defendant. Despite Stephen Ralphs's complex social history (like that of nearly all capital defendants),[5] including his dysfunctional and abusive family life, his abandonment by his drug-addicted mother, and his lengthy history of drug addiction—as a privileged insider, Madeline Kraft need only find a similarity in her own identity to dismiss Ralphs as an immoral outsider. However, it is important to note that the separation between insiders and outsiders is not a clean either/or dichotomy between moral and immoral individuals in her story. Punishing identities, as I will demonstrate throughout this book, are realized as "a pervasive two-role social process"—moral insiders and immoral outsiders "are not persons but rather perspectives" (Goffman 1963, 138). And in the case of African American capital jurors, such punishing identities or perspectives on criminals and punishment are complex and often contradictory.

Yet regardless of jurors' social status, their identities are made salient in the stories they tell. Drawing on a vast array of social (e.g., race and gender status) and cultural (e.g., media) resources, jurors' stories are often mediated by their biographical experiences (e.g., "I used drugs when I was in college"). In this way, their stories often combine multiple and sometimes contradictory realities (my life with his life with what I read about in the newspaper). However, capital jurors' accounts of their experiences often contain an underlying normative grammar that enables them to perform their official punitive role of deciding who is moral and who ultimately is not.

Institutional Constraints

The normative grammars of morality and immorality are fostered by and in the legal setting. From the moment citizens enter the courtroom, they are quizzed about their moralities and questioned by legal authorities who employ official discourses and wear ceremonial attire (black robes). Knowing that they are no longer home, citizens spend a few, often tedious, days waiting for jury selection to end. After the twelve "winners"—those who are "qualified" to serve as capital jurors[6]—have been chosen and the jury has been formed, they are then instructed about the law's official line.

In this way, the state has enlisted twelve ordinary citizens into a bizarre game that they now must play. As pawns of the killing state, they are instructed about the game's rules: They are told of their responsibility to remain impartial throughout the course of the trial, and they are reminded of their oaths of secrecy as well as the consequences if they are broken. In this way, they "know" that their roles are very important—they are to listen attentively to the often gruesome and emotionally charged evidence presented during the guilt portion of the trial, and then they are ordered to decide whether the defendant is guilty beyond a reasonable doubt.

If they convict the defendant of capital murder, they then begin the punishment phase of the trial—the trial of the defendant's life. When the emotionally intense punishment trial concludes, the jurors are either read or given their official sentencing instructions for making the life-or-death decision. Such instructions typically contain both aggravating and mitigating circumstances.[7] Jurors are reminded by the official line that they are to make an either/or decision; they are to place the defendant's life and crime into a series of jargonized legal categories of good and bad. Calculating the defendant's "death worthiness" in this way, they will subsequently determine whether he or she lives or dies.

The law's official line forces jurors to make an all-or-nothing decision; they inevitably must decide whether another human being must live or die. This experience is like no other, far removed from everyday social intercourse, and the state places awesome expectations on capital jurors. At the same time, the state's official line disciplines jurors to punish:

[T]he power to punish is not essentially different from that of curing or educating. It receives from them, and from their lesser, smaller task, a sanction from below; but one that is no less important for that, since it is the sanction of technique and rationality. (Foucault 1979, 303)

The techniques that enable capital jurors rationally to represent their decisions are produced at the intersections of their socially constructed and legally prescribed identities. The law's "solemn ritual" is the state's ever-present reminder of what juror's official duty is: "Jurors reassure themselves that the sanctions they inflict follow inevitably from the demands of neutral, disinterested legal principles, rather than from their own choice and power" (Weisberg 1983, 385). At the same time, the defendant's dangerousness or other markers of immorality inform jurors of whom they are and whom the defendant is not.

Thesis and Book Overview

In this book, I argue that capital jurors do not focus directly on defendants' racial inferiority but affect outcomes in racially significant ways in a process of at least two steps.[8]

1. They first construct a sense of themselves as a small group, and through this sense they respond to the accused and to characteristics of the accused.
2. The small-group identity they construct is one of insiders, and through it they cast the accused as an outsider. Racial and other characteristics of the accused figure in as related to outsider identity.

With my thesis now articulated, the next chapter further addresses the terrain for understanding the contemporary identity politics of crime and punishment in the United States. Subsequent sections of the book present a landscape that will prove to be very significant for making sense of capital jurors' stories of their punishment decisions.

The identity politics of crime and punishment, to which I turn in chapter 2, deals with issues of the continuing struggle for racial justice and the racialization of crime and punishment in the United States in the late twentieth century. The contemporary Supreme Court's decision to reject systematic evidence of racial discrimination in Georgia's death-sentencing protocol in *McCleskey v. Kemp*

(1987) sets the stage for the identity politics of "tough on crime" as represented in George H. W. Bush's use of the Willie Horton advertisements during the 1988 presidential campaign and in subsequent crime and punishment discourse. A study of focus group attitude change before and after the airing of the Horton ads, I argue, demonstrates a pervasive racialization of dominant moralities.

Next, I investigate the implications of the contemporary race politics of crime and punishment for studying legal discretion. Drawing on two especially noteworthy studies of prosecutorial discourse and police officer discretion provides important insights for understanding capital-sentencing discretion in practice. Finally, I argue that the identities of those "death-qualified" citizens who make the life-or-death decision are characterized by a politics of the insiders—a constellation of beliefs that ignores prevailing social and economic inequalities and, by default, blames "immoral outsiders" for their own marginality.

Focusing on jurors who resist the insiders' line, I show how the politics of the insiders, like insider identity itself, is unstable and thus may be challenged from within. Finally, I highlight who such resisters might be and the obstacles that they inevitably face in turning the tide against the majority.

In chapter 3, I begin by discussing how studying jurors' stories contributes to the social science literature on capital sentencing. I argue that the "textual turn" in the social scientific study of the death penalty is an important complement to more traditional, quantitative approaches, and I argue that the reflexive approach to theory and method that I take in the book is essential for unearthing the subtleties of the data presented. Next, I introduce the sample of jurors and the methodology, and I present the most common insiders' narratives. Drawing on the narrative methodological work of Catherine Kohler Riessman (1993), I describe in detail how the analysis presented in this book has evolved. From transcription to retranscription and editing, I draw on select examples from the analysis to highlight both my analytical progression and how "various sources shape[d] the difficult decision about how to represent oral discourse as written text" (Riessman 1993,

58). In short, this chapter seeks to elucidate how the narratives embedded in jurors' stories constitute the world of capital sentencing "as it is lived and is understood by the storyteller" (Ewick and Silbey 1998, 29).

In chapter 4, I explore how insiders mobilize and reconcile multiple identities in their stories of their punishment decisions. Drawing on a wide array of individual jurors' stories, I highlight how the narratives are mediated by insiders' personal experiences, by popular wisdom, and by the capital trial itself. In chapter 5, I focus on the voices of jurors who resist the insiders. My goal in this chapter is twofold. I wish to highlight both the near invisibility of resistant voices on death penalty juries and the challenges resisters face in overcoming the insiders.

Chapter 6 elucidates how multiple jurors from the same case represent their death-sentencing decisions along alternative narrative axes. Focusing on insider stories from various cases reveals the multiple or polyvocal normative grammars that constitute the death sentence in practice. In short, this chapter demonstrates how jurors with different social characteristics and personal experiences arrive at the decision to impose death in different yet ultimately complementary ways.

In chapter 7, I present the stories of jurors from juries in which a resister was present. Exploring how insiders handle resisters reveals both the instability of insider identities and the ominous and complex predicament resisters face in overcoming the majority.

Chapter 8 is devoted to connecting these findings to the broader world of death penalty law and society. The stories of death presented in this book reinforce the abolitionist argument that capital punishment is inherently an institution of state-sanctioned oppression. Highlighting these pervasive grammars of oppression further demonstrates the futility of contemporary death penalty reform efforts. At the same time, these findings elucidate how the continued use of the death sentence invests in prevailing dominant-subordinate race relations, thus undermining multiculturalism and a broader U.S. commitment to human rights.

Chapter 2
Race Politics, Punishment, and the Bureaucracy of Death

Defendants challenging their death sentences thus never have had to prove that impermissible considerations have actually infected sentencing decisions. We have required instead that they establish that the system under which they were sentenced posed a significant risk of such an occurrence. McCleskey's claim does differ, however, in one respect from these earlier cases: it is the first to base a challenge not on speculation about how a system might operate, but on empirical documentation of how it does operate.

> —Justice William Brennan,
> dissenting in *McCleskey v. Kemp* (1987)

E-Racing Death

On October 12, 1978, the Superior Court of Fulton County, Georgia, convicted Warren McCleskey, a black man, of robbing a furniture store and killing a white police officer. At trial, the evidence indicated that McCleskey and three accomplices planned and carried out the robbery. However, the details surrounding the murder were far from clear-cut. Responding to a silent alarm inside the store, a white police officer entered through the front door. Two gunshots were fired, with one hitting the officer in the face and killing him. After being arrested several weeks later for an unrelated offense, McCleskey confessed to participating in the robbery but denied shooting the police officer. At trial, however, the state introduced evidence suggesting that the bullet that killed the police officer matched McCleskey's gun. Two witnesses also testified that McCleskey had admitted to the shooting.

After convicting him of capital murder, the jury at McCleskey's sentencing trial found two aggravating circumstances: the murder was committed during the course of an armed robbery, and the murder was committed upon a peace officer engaged in the performance of his duties. McCleskey offered no mitigating evidence. The jury recommended that he be sentenced to death on the murder charge and to consecutive life sentences on the armed robbery charges. The trial court followed the jury's recommendation and sentenced McCleskey to death.[1]

Appealing his case to the U.S. Supreme Court, McCleskey challenged the Georgia capital-sentencing process as racially discriminatory in violation of the Eighth and Fourteenth Amendments to the U.S. Constitution. Supporting his claim, McCleskey drew on a statistical study performed by Professors David C. Baldus, George Woodworth, and Charles Pulaski Jr. (1990) that demonstrated disparities in the imposition of the death sentence in Georgia based primarily on the race of the murder victim. Focusing on more than two thousand Georgia murder cases during the 1970s, the Baldus study demonstrated that the death sentence was imposed in 22 percent of the cases involving black defendants and white victims, 8 percent of the cases involving white defendants and white victims, 1 percent of the cases involving black defendants and black victims, and 3 percent of the cases involving white defendants and black victims. Even after accounting for thirty-nine nonracial variables, the study found that defendants charged with killing white victims were 4.3 times as likely to receive a death sentence as defendants charged with killing blacks. Despite this systematic evidence, the U.S. Supreme Court voted five to four to uphold McCleskey's death sentence:

> At most, the Baldus study indicates a discrepancy that appears to correlate with race. Apparent disparities in sentencing are an inevitable part of our criminal justice system. Where the discretion that is fundamental to our

criminal process is involved, we decline to assume that what is unexplained is invidious. In light of the safeguards designed to minimize racial bias in the process, the fundamental value of jury trial in our criminal justice system, and the benefits that discretion provides to criminal defendants, we hold that the Baldus study does not demonstrate a constitutionally significant risk of racial bias affecting the Georgia capital sentencing process. (*McCleskey v. Kemp* 481 U.S. 279 [1987])

Explaining the Unexplainable

In this book, I explore the critical question that the U.S. Supreme Court in *McCleskey v. Kemp* described as "unexplainable" and thus declined to consider: How are racial identities made invidious in death penalty judgments? Unlike most studies of legal discretion, which focus on publicly available legal opinions or case outcomes, *Jurors' Stories of Death* explores the private voices of lay representatives of the state. Hearing jurors' stories, I argue, reveals a far more complex, historically situated world of legality than the *McCleskey* majority assumed, a world that is not separate from contemporary culture wars over crime and punishment policy more broadly. Focusing on death penalty judgments in the latter half of the twentieth century, this book explores a historically and institutionally mediated set of discourses utterly discounted in *McCleskey*.

Willie Horton and the Politics of White Supremacy

> Certainly no reality intrudes upon our presidential elections. They are simply fast moving fiction, empty of content at a cognitive level, but at a visceral level very powerful indeed, as the tragic election of Willie Horton to the governorship of Massachusetts demonstrated in 1988.
>
> —Gore Vidal, *Palimpsest* (1995)

Perhaps never before has a national political candidacy activated such widespread fears of crime and calls for tougher punishment as did the 1988 Bush campaign. Drawing on the major conservative legal victory in *McCleskey* a year earlier, the Horton advertisements' depiction of a poor black criminal attacking a white middle-class victim was the official coming out party for the conservatives' updated us-versus-them crime narrative, the national premiere of a revitalized identity politics of crime and punishment. By blaming Democrat Michael Dukakis for the occurrence of senseless, brutal crimes because of his alleged soft-pedaling of dangerous black offenders such as Horton, the advertisements "George Bush and Michael Dukakis on Crime" and "Governor Dukakis's Liberal Furlough Program Failed" represent both a new demonstration of Republican "tough on crime" might and an attack on Democrats as "pro–civil rights"—as betrayers of *us* and friends of *them*.[2]

The first ad showed a revolving door with running text saying that 268 convicts had escaped while on furlough and a voice-over stating that many convicts leave prison early and commit crime again. The second ad, narrated by the sister of Horton's teenaged victim, provided emotional testimony about Dukakis's record of failed furloughs and vetoes of capital punishment. Juxtaposing Dukakis's liberal punishment policies with Horton's expressionless face and a white female, the conservatives recycled "the old sham white supremacy forever wedded to and dependent upon faux black inferiority" (Morrison and Lacour 1997, xxvii).

The Horton narrative of white morality/black immorality substantially affected public consciousness of crime and punishment. Kathleen Hall Jamieson's (1992) analysis of attitude change in focus groups demonstrates how a nine-member Dallas focus group that favored Dukakis five to four in early September shifted to seven to two in favor of Bush shortly after the airing of the Horton ads. By early November, attitudes had hardened in favor of getting tough on crime and of the death penalty. The principal elements of the Horton narrative that focus group members identified were Horton's blackness and the victim's whiteness, the attendant horror of such crimes, the need for expanded use of the death penalty, Dukakis's complicity in releasing Horton, and Bush's "tough on crime" ideology. Asked to write a description of the Horton incident and to indicate their information sources for each sentence

(PN for print news, BN for televised broadcast news, RN for radio news, A for advertising, H for material overheard in conversation, and NS for not sure), one focus group member wrote,

> Willie Horton was a killer and wasn't electrocuted (H/PN). . . . He kept raping the wife (BN). He [Horton] was black and the wife was white. . . . Her husband went crazy. . . . He [the husband] still can't forgive himself. That's why he is against Dukakis (BN). Her husband says that she is afraid that he [Horton] will come back (BN/NS). He [Horton] killed a boy in a supermarket in Maryland (H). . . . I believe in the death penalty for people like that. . . . George Bush opposes gun control and favors executing Hortons (Radio—I think it was an ad). I would guess Willie Horton doesn't. (Jamieson 1992, 35)

This response contains a captivating racialized and sexualized narrative of the Horton incident. By relying on such typifications of white female domination by poor black male minorities, this respondent frames the need for an expanded death penalty using the media. Telling a tale that reveals an implicit hypersexualized, dangerous black masculinity, the respondent represents white identity as conservative and law-abiding. As in past racist myths of the black brute rapist, black masculinity is represented in this story as a predatory devil (Davis 1978; Hoch 1979), "a lascivious black male with cloven hoofs, a tail, and a huge penis capable of super-masculine exertion—an archetypal leering 'black beast from below'" (Hoch 1979, 44).[3] Indeed, the phrase "people like that" reveals the broader resonance of the Horton story for the white middle class: The liberals care more about the civil rights of poor black male hypersexualized predators who are stalking white middle-class women than about moral, law-abiding middle-class whites.

The devastating political effectiveness of the Horton ads also becomes especially apparent when analyzed over time. Jamieson's study demonstrates how focus group members became resistant to evidence that might debunk the accusations against Dukakis. Statistics documenting the overall success of the Massachusetts furlough program, as well as statistics from the federal government showing higher rates of early release and recidivism in California under Governor Ronald Reagan, provoked one group member to respond, "You can't change my mind with all of that. . . . When you support the death penalty, the really bad ones get killed. That's . . . the problem with . . . liberals" (Jamieson 1992, 31–32). Another focus group member dismissed statistical evidence: "We should ship all our criminals to the college liberals in College Station . . . or Austin [Texas]. . . . Crime's not statistics, honey" (Jamieson 1992, 31–32). These responses indicate the depth and persistence of white fears of so-called predatory black crime. (See chap. 3 for a more detailed discussion of this topic.)

Contesting "Tough on Crime"

The identity politics of crime and punishment in the public arena has a long history dating back to the Nixon campaign and presidency (Beckett 1997; Beckett and Sasson 2000; Sasson 1995; Scheingold 1984). Most telling, however, has been the compliance of the Democratic Party (Hitchens 2000). Indeed, the Left's assent to the war on crime is typified most starkly in its endorsement of the conservative-led Violent Crime Control and Law Enforcement Act of 1994.[4] Most recently, the liberal hesitation to contest the Right may best be represented in the reluctance to endorse national death-penalty-moratorium legislation despite the recent discoveries of dozens of erroneous death sentences across the United States (Scheck, Neufeld, and Dwyer 2000).[5]

In response to liberal acquiescence to conservative-driven crime-and-punishment policies, a new and important theoretical dialogue and sociolegal critique has recently emerged (Bell 1987; Butler 1997; Carbado 1999; Crenshaw et al. 1996; Haney-López 1996; Lawrence 1987; Matsuda 1989; Morrison and Lacour 1997). In addition to contesting blatant anti-civil-rights measures (e.g., the disparity between federal sentences for crack and powder cocaine) characterizing the late twentieth century, critical race theory focuses on the limitations of traditional liberal notions of civil rights. Traditional liberalism has often viewed equal protection as sufficiently corrective (Pyle 1999), and many conservatives have seen it as reverse discrimination (D'Souza 1995); in contrast, critical race theory calls attention to the inherent flaws in such reforms.

In short, the liberal equal-protection project in the context of criminal justice sees racism's trees but fails to see its forests. By focusing on individual acts of racial discrimination rather than the systemic effects on those discriminated against, such a project only preserves and reinforces or, at the very least, ignores the roots of such disparities. Such a narrow interpretation of racial discrimination in the criminal justice system remains relevant in the context of contemporary civil rights. Indeed, cases such as *McCleskey* continue to rely heavily on what Alan David Freedman (1978) calls a "perpetrator perspective" of racial discrimination:

> The concept of "racial discrimination" may be approached from the perspective of either its victim or perpetrator. . . . From the victim's perspective, racial discrimination describes those conditions of actual social existence as a member of a perpetual underclass. . . . The perpetrator perspective sees racial discrimination not as conditions, but as actions, or a series of actions, inflicted on the victim by the perpetrator. (1051–52)

Thus, from the perpetrator perspective, racism is present only when an actor engages in an act of racial discrimination against another individual or group: there is no racism outside of a specifically, intentionally racist act.[6] Such a model dominates the contemporary criminal justice system and thus has had deleterious effects on communities of color (D. Cole 1999; Mann and Zatz 1998; Mauer 1999; Tonry 1997; Walker, Spohn, and DeLone 2000). In addition to persistent institutional discrimination, another, perhaps more sinister, ideological function is revealed: such ideology invests in white middle-class supremacy. In this way, the death penalty reinforces "the inherent inferiority of blacks and the equally fallacious assumptions of the superiority of whites by whites" (Crenshaw 1997, 104).[7]

Punishment and Identity

To properly contextualize how the death penalty invests in racial identities, we must first consider the complexities of punishment as a bureaucratic apparatus of "enlightened" state government. Perhaps the most insightful discussion of such complexities is Michel Foucault's classic *Discipline and Punish* (1979). Foucault eloquently demonstrates the simultaneous development of moral and bureaucratic identities in the penal apparatus and society more broadly. For Foucault, the movement from public executions to private institutions coincided with the birth of the Enlightenment and the subsequent bureaucratization of the social and thus moral domains. The growth of the material economy institutionalized both social discipline and social hierarchy at the same time that it normalized legal control of the body politic. The entrenchment of bureaucratized disciplinary power and control had important consequences for the meaning of *crime* and *punishment*.

> As a result, a certain significant generality moved between the least irregularity and the greatest crime; it was no longer the offence, the attack on the common interest, it was the departure from the norm, the anomaly; it was this that haunted the school, the court, the asylum or the prison. It generalized in the sphere of meaning the function that the carceral generalized in the sphere of tactics. Replacing the adversary of the sovereign, the social enemy was transformed into deviant, who brought with him one another. In effect, the great continuity of the carceral system throughout the law and its sentences gives a sort of legal sanction to the disciplinary mechanisms, to the decisions of judgments that they enforce. (Foucault 1979, 301–2)

Foucault's conception of the carceral sheds light on modern society's increased reliance on law in reinforcing dominant moralities. Modern punishment's institutionalized routines reveal how morality itself is bureaucratized. While Foucault presents a fascinating analysis of the disciplinary regimes of bureaucratized punishment, he does not investigate how discipline is explicitly realized at the individual level (i.e., the discretionary judgments of legal actors).

Problematizing identities at the individual level is especially important in an analysis of discretionary legal action, including capital sentencing. Indeed, such a context leads to a central question: How are identities embedded in the implicitly moral decision to invoke the law, including the death sentence?

Jurors' Stories of Death

Identities are interwoven in legal consciousness; legal action is not a clean and mechanistic process of categorization. For example, a lower-class black person living in a marginalized community may have a very different position on the death penalty than a black person who lives in a middle-class neighborhood. They may also have very different moral orientations, because "morality is bound to a sense of self, helps determine our sense of others, and then becomes the grounds to legitimate identities" (Oberweis and Musheno 2001, 64).

Moral consciousness of law is elucidated in the stories that give meaning to legal actors' identities at the same time that such identities give meaning to *law*. In this way, state agents such as capital jurors employ narratives that simultaneously constitute taken-for-granted understandings of the agents' identities as moral insiders and constitute defendants or victims as immoral outsiders.

Austin Sarat's study of racialized stories of violence in prosecutorial arguments in death penalty trials demonstrates the nexus of violence and identity in capital trial narratives. Problematizing the prosecution's argument—"We have a right," the prosecutor claimed, "to be vindicated and protected"—Sarat elucidates how such narrating of violence as offensive to dominant moralities simultaneously serves to reinforce racial essentialism in death trials.

"We" is both an inclusive and a violent naming, a naming fraught with racial meaning. Who is included in the "we"? While this "we" reaches from this world to the next as a remembrance of and identification with [the white victim], at the same time, it makes the black [defendant] an outsider in a community that needs protection from people like him. It excludes him by claiming law as an entitlement against him. Law's violence is necessary both to vindicate and protect "us" from him. (1993, 49)

Studies in other legal contexts demonstrate the interconnectedness of law and identity. Trish Oberweis and Michael Musheno's (2001) fascinating study of legal consciousness among street-level bureaucrats persuasively reveals how moral decision making is inextricably bound up in state actors' historically specific, institutionally constrained identities. Focusing on the stories of police officers and social services administrators, Oberweis and Musheno provide a fascinating window into how multiple identities constitute discretionary judgments. Having respondents sketch stories about how their perspectives of morality informed their decision making, these authors present an illuminating perspective on the interconnectedness of identity, morality, and the law in action. Describing the arrest of a woman identified as pregnant, a prostitute, and an alcoholic, a white police officer, Clinton Hinkley, stated,

She blew a .225 [on a breath alcohol test], which is over twice the legal limit. . . . She was real happy about it and didn't think anything about the fact that she was drinking. She thought that she was doing good because she was cutting down. That right there caused me a lot of problems, especially because I have a seven-month-old baby. That just really bothers me. My wife didn't touch a single sip of alcohol, didn't take any medications or anything, just because she didn't want any possible thing wrong with the baby. And this one's going to grow up with a mother who doesn't even know who the father is of her unborn child and she's out here drinking up. . . .

The only way you can do anything about it is if they make abortions illegal. My understanding is that there are a lot of people who get home abortions and have their own ways of aborting their children. Some of which is through alcohol and drugs, so it's just a form of abortion. That way if you have prostitutes or people out there that are doing drugs or alcohol while they're pregnant, then we can force them into custody for the term of the pregnancy to keep them from abusing the baby. . . . The only other way to help prevent this is to give all drug addicted females or female prostitutes a hysterectomy. (Oberweis and Musheno 2001, 75)

Officer Hinkley's story powerfully demonstrates how morality is constructed at the intersections of experiential, institutional, and historically specific identities. As a "good parent" in the late twentieth century, a white working-class male mobilizes the prolife politics of gendered immorality.[8] Borrowing from conservative stories of "welfare queens" and "immoral single mothers," Hinkley as both officer and "good parent" wants to "force them into custody." In other words, the female suspect represents to him a breed of immoral outsiders that has taken full advantage of "liberal" abortion policies ("The only way you can do anything about it is if they make abortions illegal") and therefore must be punished harshly. Framing his arrest story in the context of his privilege vis-à-vis his wife's pregnancy, he, by implication, ignores the female suspect's marginality. Officer Hinkley mobilizes a story of individual responsibility[9] and thus blames the "dishonest," "morally reprehensible" woman for her impoverished and marginalized identity ("She thought that she was doing good"). At the same time, he mobilizes his institutional role as law enforcer "to enforce his moral view to the extent that he can, with rather significant consequences for the woman involved" (Oberweis and Musheno 2001, 75).

Experiential and political resources are historically and politically mediated as legal action. In this way, death penalty judgments are simultaneously legal and social projects. The death sentence is made "legal" by jurors' experiences and beliefs about morality and immorality. Indeed, deciding death is implicitly about representations of self and Other. In the latter part of the twentieth century, the dominant conception of criminals relied implicitly on the representations of the economically and racially marginalized as immoral outsiders.[10]

Bureaucratizing Identity and Death

From this perspective, capital punishment is thus the preeminent manifestation of what the great social psychologist George H. Mead conceived as punishment's morally reflexive social function: the sentence of death unequivocally pronounces the condemned as outside the moral order. At the same time, the death sentence has an implicitly pedagogical function—it teaches and reteaches the moral majority what it means to be inside. From Mead's perspective, having the death penalty in the United States today actually continues to foster or promote the production *and* reproduction of racial identities.

> As long as the social organization is dominated by the attitude of hostility the individuals or groups who are the objectives of this organization will remain enemies. It is quite impossible psychologically to hate the sin and love the sinner. We are very much given to cheating ourselves in this regard. (Mead 1918, 600)

The racialized identity politics that pervade crime and punishment discourse in American culture thus has meaning for punishment in practice. However, such discourses are, as the Willie Horton incident demonstrates, powerful political technologies, but they reveal very little about the actual doings of the private discretionary moments that constitute punishment practice. Michael Dukakis's decision to furlough Willie Horton was obviously far more complex than the Bush campaign would have the public believe. An understanding of the private domain of penal practice depends on disclosing the *how* of discretionary power rather than on examining the public, often politically distorted, intentions of discretionary state actors. This study approaches this subject from this perspective, concentrating on the stories of jurors from particular cases. In this way, I argue that who jurors are has much to do with how they will see particular defendants or victims and how jurors will make life-or-death decisions.

Capital Punishment at All Costs

McCleskey v. Kemp and the Horton spectacle typify America's public story of death penalty law and society: Punishment is more important than racial equity and the protection of defendants' due process rights in the criminal justice system. Thus, in addition to rejecting the Baldus study's compelling evidence of racial discrimination in death-sentencing outcomes, the Supreme Court does not require proportionate review, deregulated guided discretion, allowed the inclusion of victim-impact testimony during the punishment phase, and thoroughly gutted posthabeas relief for the condemned (for a review, see Steiker and Steiker 1998). Responding to the late Justice Harry Blackmun's dissent and classic decision to no longer "tinker with the machinery of death" in denying certiorari in *Callins v. Collins* (1994), Justice Antonin Scalia's concurrence with the majority vividly exposes the Supreme Court majority's vengeance-driven punishment-at-all-costs jurisprudence.

> How enviable a quiet death by lethal injection compared with [the murder of a child]! If the people . . . conclude that justice requires such brutal deaths to be avenged by capital punishment; the creation of false, untextual and unhistorical contradictions within "the Court's Eighth Amendment jurisprudence" should not prevent them. (*Callins v. Collins* 510 U.S. 1141 [1994])[11]

The "people" to whom Justice Scalia refers are most certainly the conservative white middle-class constituencies that were mobilized during the Horton spectacle. If former liberal Supreme Court clerk Edward P. Lazarus is correct in his incendiary tome, *Closed Chambers* (1998), George H. W. Bush's defeat of Michael Dukakis was a catalyst for the contemporary Court's punishment-at-all costs jurisprudence.

> With Bush's victory, all the liberal Pollyannaish scenarios for holding the line at the Court vanished like so many rainbows at sundown. You could read in every one of our faces the same grim calculation: could Brennan, Marshall, and Blackmun—each over eighty and all ill in their own ways—possibly

hold on for another four years? Not a soul among us thought they could, which meant that the steady pace of our defeats would soon become a wholesale rout. In our corners of the building, every day felt like Dunkirk was that much closer and our job was simply to salvage for some distant future those scattered parts of the liberal legacy resilient enough to endure. (279–80)

The current antiliberal politics of punishment at all costs governs death penalty law and society: Execute the "immoral," often non-white, outsiders.

Studying the Death-Qualified

As collusion between conservative politics and law, death qualification is more than a legal procedure for weeding out "unqualified" citizens from the pool of potential capital jurors; it is a means for mobilizing a group that can be expected to act in accordance with the dominant politicolegal ideology.

The ability to give the death sentence is synonymous with holding a set of beliefs that represents economically and racially marginalized capital defendants or victims as immoral outsiders. At the same time, capital jurors employ, in often contradictory and fragmented voices, this ideology to represent themselves as moral insiders. The insider-outsider distinction is extremely fragile—all jurors see capital murder as immoral but, depending on who they are, struggle to make sense of their decision to impose the life sentence or the death sentence. From this perspective, the public story of punishment at all costs as articulated by the Supreme Court becomes, however transmuted, the politico-punitive capital of the insiders. As both representatives of popular sovereignty and bureaucratic agents of the state, jurors mobilize an institutionally mediated common sense of the outsider's punishment. Death penalty consciousness is realized in the ways jurors simultaneously manipulate moralities and the identities of those targeted for punishment under the law.

Capital jurors hold disproportionately punitive orientations toward crime and criminal justice (Steiner 1999; see also appendix

B), are more likely to be conviction prone (Fitzgerald and Ellsworth 1984), are more likely to hold racial stereotypes (Haney, Hurtado, and Vega 1994), and are more likely to be pro-prosecution (Steiner 1999; see also appendix B). In this way, "death qualification" is more than a bureaucratic process that the state employs to ensure that capital jurors will abide by death penalty law; it is an institutionalized proxy for ensuring that death penalty judgments will be infused with jurors' politicolegal consciousness.

"Death Qualification" in Theory and Practice

According to official procedures governing death penalty trials, *death qualification* refers to a process during jury selection during which judges and attorneys evaluate a prospective juror's ability to impose the death sentence. Evaluating a venire person's ability to punish typically involves two steps. First, members of the venire are questioned about whether they can consider both a life and a death sentence. Those who oppose the death sentence are, in effect, "unqualified" and struck for cause. Second, to insure that the guilt and punishment decisions are made separately, death-qualified jurors are instructed to make the life-or-death decision only after hearing the evidence, the arguments, and the instructions for making that decision. They are theoretically required to maintain their impartiality in making both the guilt and the punishment decisions.

Whether death qualification in theory comports with practice is another matter. An imposing collection of empirical studies documents that death qualification leads to a penchant for conviction (Thompson 1989) and a predisposition for imposing death (Bowers, Sandys, and Steiner 1998).[12] However, even in the face of such systematic evidence, the Supreme Court has recently abandoned its long-standing concerns about such matters of fundamental fairness.

We will assume for purposes of this opinion that the studies are both methodologically valid and adequate to establish that "death qualification" in fact produces juries somewhat more "conviction-prone" than "non–death qualified" juries. We hold, nonetheless, that the Constitution does not prohibit the States from "death qualifying" juries in capital cases. (*Lockhart v. McCree* 476 U.S. 162, 173 [1986])

Research on the death-qualification process also demonstrates the disproportionate exclusion of racial minorities from capital-sentencing juries. Focusing on voir dire questioning, researchers find that prospective African Americans are more likely to question the efficacy of the death penalty and are subsequently struck for cause in disproportionate numbers (Haney, Hurtado, and Vega 1994). Other studies establish a connection between various measures of racial prejudice and support for severe criminal punishments, including the death penalty (Barkan and Cohn 1994; Sweeney and Haney 1992).

The Death-Qualified as Insiders

Death qualification is a legal fiction. Ability to impose death is a proxy for conviction proneness, predisposition to punishment, and racial bias. Ability to impose death is also linked to holding a constellation of political beliefs. Marshalling this empirical evidence in her extremely insightful book, *Making Crime Pay,* Katherine Beckett observes,

> In sum, attitudes regarding crime and punishment are inextricably bound up with race and racial attitudes; opposition to racial and social reform is crucial in accounting for white support for law and order policies. (1997, 85)[13]

The ability to impose the death sentence can thus be viewed as a surrogate for a belief system implicated in the political production and reproduction of dominant-subordinate racial identities. Two of the most effective polarizing discourses in this respect are opposition to welfare and, as the Horton spectacle so vividly demonstrated, calls for punitive criminal justice policies. One excellent example is the conservative attack on "welfare queens"[14] and the unprecedented targeting of disproportionately poor African American and Latino "crack demons."

Crack was a godsend to the Right. They used it and the drug issue as an ideological fig leaf to place over the unsightly urban ills that had increased markedly under Reagan administration social and economic policies. "The drug problem" served conservative politicians as an all-purpose scapegoat. They could blame an array of problems on the deviant individuals and then expand the nets of social control to imprison those people for causing the problems. (Reinarman and Levine 1997, 38)

The end of Aid to Families with Dependent Children in effect legitimized the view of the economically and racially underprivileged as patently immoral, dangerous, and oversexualized. The targeting of such aggrieved groups by political elites can thus be seen as making critical investments in insider identities. As Frank Munger, writing about the making and remaking of the contemporary poor and unpoor, has cogently observed,

Stereotyping the poor creates values for and reinforces the identity of the nonpoor by justifying avoidance of the "dangers" posed by the poor, by making the nonpoor feel superior as possessors of traits that are distinct from the traits of the poor, by reinforcing the moral values of the nonpoor, by creating a class of popular-culture villains from which moral lessons (and commercial sales) can be derived, by contributing to spatial stigmatization that justifies patterns of exclusion and social control. (1998, 959–60)

The criminal justice system's targeting of poor whites and marginalized racial and ethnic minorities invests in a common sense of racial insider and outsider identities. These investments take two forms. First, long-standing seek-and-destroy tactics—arresting, incarcerating, and disfranchising racial and ethnic minorities— eliminate the competition faced by a predominantly white labor market, thereby controlling groups perceived as economic threats to whites (Musto 1973).[15] Second, and more germane to my argument here, by erroneously reinforcing outsiders as criminal and dangerous, privileged insider identities are similarly constituted as law-abiding and innocent. Although class, race, and ethnic status are social and cultural constructions—as opposed to biological determinants—they speciously become proxies for who is moral and who is immoral. (For a more detailed discussion of the politics of the insiders, see appendix A.)

Putting Chapter 2 in Perspective

Studying capital jurors' decisions is obviously a complex, multi-contextual endeavor. Race politics, punishment, and bureaucratic constraints provide a vivid set of expectations for how death-qualified citizens will actually "do" death as capital jurors. At the theoretical core of this endeavor, I am obviously putting forth a claim about the nature of social reality—how we know what we know about our surroundings. However, while social science scholars typically make one ontological commitment after another, I have resisted this temptation. I believe that the political, cultural, and legal resources available to capital jurors invite both objective and subjective interpretations of the bizarre social world in which the jurors find themselves (a room full of strangers asked to decide whether to take the life of another stranger). Put simply, this book assumes that the world of the capital juror is separate and can be observed, measured, and isolated. At the same time, I have discovered that this world is clearly colored by human—wholly subjective—experiences.[16]

Chapter 3
Story Worlds of Death

Chapter 2 presented a challenging and complex theoretical landscape for investigating the experiences of death-qualified capital-sentencing jurors. However, it is possible to ground this analysis of jurors' stories with the following broad question: How are the social and politically constructed identities of citizens mediated by their legal roles as capital jurors? In the previous chapter, I demonstrated how often-conflicting sources of knowledge problematize any prospect of a clean analysis of how capital jurors' follow the law. The doings of death are far more complex than drawing on obviously racialized images of Willie Horton to argue for the death penalty. At the same time, the doings of death are obviously more complicated than whether jurors understand their sentencing instructions (Bentele and Bowers 2001; Bowers, Sandys, and Steiner 2001; Luginbuhl and Howe 1995; Sandys 1995).

In contrast, capital jurors are presented with all the gory details and complexities of an actual murder involving not only the defendant but the testimonies of many different witnesses and the often emotionally and political charged stories of prosecutors and defense attorneys. In this way, capital jurors are asked to simultaneously defend public boundaries, reinforce private selves, and publicly—in the name of the state, as a death-qualified juror—decide whether to condemn the Othered to death. Jurors' stories thus often contain taken-for-granted understandings of who I am, who I think you are, and how we should proceed. When jurors evaluate who a defendant or victim is and whether he[1] deserves to live or die, identities are both confirmed and resisted. In short, details of jurors' stories reveal a complex, variable process.[2]

The Sample of Jurors

The sample of former capital jurors comes from the Capital Jury Project (CJP), a national study of the experiences of citizens who served as jurors on death penalty cases. I coded, transcribed, and analyzed this data for more than seven years (1992–2000) as both an undergraduate and a graduate student under the guidance of the CJP's Principal Investigator, William J. Bowers of Northeastern University. The CJP incorporates a three-stage sampling design. First, states were chosen to represent the principal variation in guided discretion. Full capital trials since 1988 with both guilt and sentencing phases were selected to provide balanced coverage between cases that resulted in life sentences and those that resulted in death sentences.[3] Moreover, investigators in each state stratified and balanced the representation of sentencing outcomes in terms of regions within the state or of urban and rural locations. While interviews were sought with four jurors from each case, investigators in some places conducted interviews with less than or more than four jurors.[4]

The interviews were conducted by a consortium of law and social science personnel. Jurors were asked a myriad of questions about their trial experiences and their broader attitudes toward crime and the criminal justice system (see appendix B). To encourage respondents to relate stories about their experiences, interviewers explicitly asked jurors to tell about important moments during the trial and deliberations and about their impressions of the defendant. These questions sought to enable jurors to construct their responses in their own ways. For example, when asked to tell about their sentencing decisions, jurors would often give a chronological accounting of what the jury did to reach its punishment decision (e.g., "First we took a vote to see where everybody stood on punishment"). While some jurors told stories of their decisions only from this perspective, others broke from a strict accounting of the jury's decision-making protocol to tell a story about other experiences. Because jurors had the leeway to answer as they saw fit, in many instances their stories emerged when I least expected it. For example, in response to their impressions of the defendant, many jurors told extended stories about problems with the criminal justice system or compared the defendant to other high-profile murderers (e.g., Charles Manson).

The interviews typically took place at the juror's home. All of the interviews lasted between three and four hours, and most were tape-recorded. The transcription of jurors' responses was a massive and lengthy effort. The preparation of the data for analysis has taken the better part of a decade. In this time, dozens of student assistants have transcribed what is now in excess of 800 transcribed interviews. Students worked approximately 10–15 hours per week for a minimum of five years to get most of the transcription done. I managed a portion of this transcription effort after I took over for Patricia Igo as Associate Research Scientist on the project.

In approaching the narrative analysis, I first coded for subsequent features that struck me as important. In some instances, transcribers had inserted exclamation marks at the end of sentences or wrote parenthetical notes that described jurors' reactions to a particular question (e.g., "Juror seems annoyed by this question"; "Juror got very serious when answering"). To better orient myself to these comments, I referred back to the tape recordings whenever possible.

In a way similar to Riessman's (1993, 57) methodological approach, research assistants were instructed to transcribe each juror's response in its entirety, even if it did not directly answer the question that had been asked. Answering a closed-ended question about how long respondents believed first-degree murderers in their states not sentenced to death spent in prison, many jurors told broader stories about America's "broken justice system." In response to being asked how the jury made its punishment decision, Leslie Odom, a white homemaker, said,

> I read the papers every day, and I'd say 60 percent to 70 percent of the crime committed in my area is committed by people who've been in prison and got out early on several different occasions. We have had quite a few murders, and early release is the cause of it.

From this response, it is clear how this juror's response cannot be assumed. The thing to be explained must be discovered, not taken for granted. In other words, what is the juror saying in this response? Why does she tell a story about inmates being released early from prison in her community? The more I scrutinized jurors' responses in the context of my prior theoretical expectations regarding death penalty consciousness (see chap. 2), the more features of discourse "jumped out" (Riessman 1993, 57) at me.

My interests in critical race theory in the context of Erving Goffman's conception of identity as a "pervasive two-role social process" (1963, 138) played a central role throughout the analysis as well.[5] For example, in response to an open-ended question about her impressions of the defendant, in this case an African American male, Sheila Brooks, a white college-educated hairdresser, stated,

> I saw the defendant as a very typical product of the lower socioeconomic black group who grew up with no values, no ideals, no authority, no morals, no leadership, and this has come down from generation to generation. And that was one of the problems we had, for me, and in the jury. Because some of the jurors were looking at him as your average white kid: he wasn't a white kid. He came from a totally different environment. I'm just saying that he was the one that was the defendant. And I just saw him as a loser from day one, as soon as he was born into that environment and into that set of people who basically were into drugs, alcohol, illegitimacy, AIDS, the whole nine yards. This kid didn't have a chance. That's how I saw the defendant. And there are ten thousand others like him out there, which is very tragic.

Sheila Brooks's response is obviously more than a simple description of the defendant. She tells a rich and detailed story that draws on themes of racial identity, morality, and tragedy. (See chap. 4 for more detailed analysis of Brooks's comments.) However, from Goffmanian and critical race perspectives, her story raises several fascinating questions: How does identifying the defendant's blackness enable her to understand her own white identity? What is the purpose of telling a story of her fellow jurors' reactions to the defendant? How does her use of ambiguous identifiers such as "that," "totally different," "that set of people," and the "whole nine yards" help her to make sense of the defendant's identity? What does the statement, "There are ten thousand others like him out there, which is very tragic" say about the role of tragedy[6] in Sheila Brooks's story?

The development of these theoretically grounded questions in combination with my analytical refinement of jurors' stories was a long and painstaking process. Through numerous rounds of retranscribing and revising, I clarified my interpretations of jurors' stories. Moreover, I ultimately made the difficult decision about how to represent respondents' discourse in the texts presented here. "Determining where a narrative begins and ends and the listener/questioner's place in producing it are textual as well as analytic issues" (Riessman 1993, 58).

Jurors' Responses as Moral Justifications

> Justifications are accounts in which one accepts responsibility for the act in question, but denies the pejorative quality associated with it.
>
> —Marvin B. Scott and Stanford M. Lyman, "Accounts" (1968)

Capital jurors' stories can often be heard explicitly as justifications for how and why they made particular decisions. Recounting their experiences, they employ moral justifications as a storytelling technique to persuade the interviewer. However, I strongly suspect that storytelling among jurors at the time they made their sentencing decisions was justified by the same or similar means. In the context of taking on this foreign role of juror, respondents' stories elucidate how they present themselves to one another in particularized ways, often with the goal of establishing their identities and moral views. At the juror level, this becomes quite evident when viewed in the context of the interviewer-respondent exchanges. In the following example, a juror justifies his anger toward the defendant.

INTERVIEWER: Yes or no, did you have the following thoughts or feelings about the defendant? You felt anger or rage toward him.

JUROR: I was angry because hundreds of thousands of people are like this throughout the country. They cause all this aggravation and money to be spent on the court system. It's just ridiculous! It's wasting my time.

INTERVIEWER: Yes or no, did you feel contempt or hatred for the defendant's family?

JUROR: I don't hate anyone. It's the same bullshit that never stops. There's too much of it. Our welfare system makes these people—our dollars we give them. It's terrible and awful.

This exchange reveals how the asking of seemingly straightforward "yes or no" questions can invite some respondents to tell personal stories that justify why they acted the way they did. "I don't hate anyone" elucidates the negotiation between interviewer and interviewee. Instead of answering "No" in response to the question about whether he had "contempt or hatred for the defendant's family," this juror treats the question as a personal affront; he tells a highly emotional and angry ("It's the same bullshit that never stops") story about America's "broken" welfare system.

In sum, my methodological approach to the analysis began with identifying what jurors were saying in the context of their decisions. Expanding beyond a literal interpretation of what was on the page, I began to notice consistencies in the way jurors made sense in their stories, including the taken-for-granted normative grammars of both speaker and listener. By privileging the telling of jurors' stories, I made subsequent analytical interpretations. Indeed, the more I returned to the data, the more I began to connect the particularities of jurors' stories to broader political, cultural, and bureaucratic interpretations of identity, morality, and punishment.

An Exploratory Approach

Because the CJP interview protocol did not specifically ask respondents to tell stories about their broader views on identity and punishment, I took a more exploratory approach to investigating their open-ended responses. Specifically, I have not tried to obtain a representative sample that can be generalized to all jurors in penalty trials, nor, as I have done in a more focused previous study (Fleury-Steiner 2001), to focus on juror and defendant racial characteristics. To learn about the thinking of jurors here, I have sought out interviews where jurors provide the richest detail and clearest insights about the underlying decision process. I believe that these stories reveal the fundamental process involved in jurors' punishment decisions and I advance this argument explicitly so that future research can provide a more rigorous and exacting test.

The data presented are thus the ones I found most helpful for exploring jurors' explanations for deciding to impose the death penalty in marginalized white and minority (both Latino and especially African American) defendant cases. They are the cases that best enable me to tell the story the data reveal. As table 1 shows, the sample of 57 jurors from 26 cases for this research is like the larger sample of jurors from which it was drawn in most respects, with some notable exceptions that reflect the purposes of this investigation. In particular, three of four jurors (78.2%) in this sample come from African American and Latino defendant cases as compared to less than half (44.5%) in the full sample. Additionally, close to half of these jurors (43.9%) come from the two states of California and Texas as compared to less than a quarter (21.6%) in the full sample. Both of these departures from representativeness reflect the need in this research to include jurors from minority defendant cases, especially from the relatively rare Latino defendant cases. Furthermore, in order to investigate the ways identity comes to bear in cases when jurors decide not to impose the death sentence, 7 of the 26 cases I present ended with a life sentence.

With respect to standard demographic characteristics, this sample is very similar in jurors' race, but slightly more female than the pool of cases from which it was drawn. This sample is also better educated and more affluent than jurors in the full sample. Where they appear, however, these demographic differences are not much more than 10 percentage points. No doubt, some of these differ-

TABLE 1.   The Sample of 57 Jurors Used in This Study
Compared with the Full Sample of 1,198 Jurors in the Capital
Jury Project (CJP)

	This Sample	Full CJP Sample
Juror Sex		
Male	37.5	49.1
Female	62.5	50.9
N	(56)	(1,136)
Juror Race		
White	86.7	85.7
Black	8.9	9.7
Hispanic	—	2.7
Asian	—	.3
Other	5.4	.6
N	(56)	(1,133)
Juror Family Income		
< $19,999 per year	24.5	31.6
$20K–$29,999K per year	26.4	30.0
$30K–$49,999K per year	24.8	22.5
$50K–$74,999K per year	24.5	15.6
> $75K per year	22.0	14.8
N	(53)	(1,038)
Defendant Race		
White	20.0	54.4
Black	49.1	38.8
Hispanic	29.1	5.7
Other	1.8	1.1
N	(55)	(1,131)
Victim Race		
White	51.9	75.8
Black	27.8	17.4
Hispanic	16.7	4.8
Other	3.7	2.0
N	(54)	(1,123)
State Where Trial Was Held		
Alabama	1.8	5.1
California	28.1	11.9

TABLE 1.—*Continued*

	This Sample	Full CJP Sample
Florida	1.8	10.2
Georgia	10.5	6.2
Indiana	—	8.9
Kentucky	3.5	9.7
Louisiana	3.5	2.5
Missouri	3.5	5.2
North Carolina	12.3	6.7
Pennsylvania	7.0	6.1
South Carolina	8.8	9.6
Tennessee	—	4.3
Texas	15.8	9.7
Virginia	3.5	3.9
N	(57)	(1,141)

ences reflect my own preference for extensive narrative accounts provided by patient, articulate, and forthcoming respondents.

The Cases

Given that the American criminal justice system and the death penalty continues to be infected with racialized discourses (e.g., Mann and Zatz 2001), I paid particular attention to African American defendant cases. While there were few jurors interviewed from Latino defendant cases, I do analyze one case (Pedro Arenas) in detail in chapter 7.

I did not analyze jurors' chronicles of technical matters, such as how they picked the jury foreperson or the like. My focus on jurors' justifications limited my analysis to two broad organizing questions: Are the identities of state agents and those they judge represented in jurors' stories? What do such stories tell us about America's culture of racial inequality more broadly? I thus could not explicitly explore whether or not jurors "follow the law" in capital cases. However, I believe that the stories I present are quite compelling for what they reveal about the subtle intersections of race, identity, and the role of state punishment in American society.

While I found no explicit reference to race in cases involving white defendants, I discovered that jurors did tell stories invoking class marginality and other alternative outsider tropes. I analyze white defendant cases in chapter 7 (Donald Carson) and chapter 8 (Barry Lawrence).

The Stories That Insiders Tell

What narratives do the insiders mobilize in their stories of their sentencing decisions and in their descriptions of defendants? While these narratives are by no means mutually exclusive—indeed, they often overlap and reinforce one another—they are nearly always politically, culturally, and institutionally situated (see chap. 2). That is to say, they vary by both the identities of the actors involved (jurors, defendants, victims, witnesses, and so forth) and the circumstances surrounding the crime or trial. Thus, to clarify the utility of each narrative, it is important to describe them separately.

The stories of those who strongly justify their decision to impose death (what I have termed the insiders) often contain variations on the narratives heard in the recent culture wars over crime and welfare (see chap. 2). Framed in the context of the jury's decision to impose punishment, insider tales often combine political, cultural, and bureaucratic resources with personal and trial experiences. Combining these resources with official, institutionally prescribed responsibilities as jurors, these stories are windows into death penalty discretion in practice.

The Story of Individual Responsibility

Jurors' stories of their experiences are incorporated into their evaluations of defendants' responsibility for crimes. Telling stories of experiences with crime or drug abuse, jurors rationalize defendants' struggles as thinly veiled "excuses." Bonnie Mayer, a white homemaker, sentenced to death Cal Swenson, a white male who raped and strangled a white female. According to Mayer,

I lived in a poor community, and I knew of families that were not too far from the defendant's family's level of poverty. They had difficult lives. They didn't have a lot of personal possessions. During the trial, the psychologist brought up that Cal didn't have shoes or clothes to wear—both the lack of these things he had growing up and the fact that he didn't have a mother and father in the house to discipline him and to really love him. I believe that really did affect the defendant. But I had seen other people in poverty that did not go on to lead a life of crime. That's no excuse. I'm sorry. I felt very bad that he had no life, but that's no reason to do what he did.

Throughout this book, it will become evident that insider stories are replete with variations on the idea that poverty is no excuse for crime. The dominant crime discourse of the Right made most salient in President George H. W. Bush's declaration of war against "the tendency to blame crime on society rather than the criminal" (1989) is often a potent narrative in these stories.

The Story of a Broken Justice System

Jurors describe a failed welfare state or the obvious inability of the prison system to rehabilitate criminals. Drawing on tough-on-crime, conservative rhetoric, they tell stories of a failed liberal state. Alternatively, they tell stories of a revolving-door prison system that cannot be entrusted to ensure a life sentence. In a word, jurors "know" that "life doesn't mean life." Broken justice stories are imported from newspapers or from what jurors have heard from acquaintances who are legal professionals (lawyers or corrections officials). Jurors impose the death sentence, by default, as "obviously, the only decision we could make." Cindy Barlow, a white schoolteacher, cited her boyfriend's mother and common knowledge as her official sources.

We were discussing how our prisons are so overcrowded now. It's already a fact that there are people being released that would normally have been in prison a lot longer. I mean, if it gets worse, who knows what's going to happen in the next ten, fifteen, or twenty-five years in our prisons? My boyfriend's mother works at the Department of Corrections, and, I mean, just knowing what you hear—you know, street talk. Everybody knows that you can commit a murder these days and be out in no time. It really alarms me.

Like the focus group respondents in Kathleen Hall Jamieson's (1992) study of voting behavior (see chap. 2), the captivating tale of a broken justice system that "favors" defendants over victims is mobilized in jurors' decisions to impose the death sentence.

Only a Recommendation

Jurors deny responsibility for their sentencing decisions, framing their choices as merely "recommendations." Focusing explicitly on their roles as jurors, they tell stories of their sentencing decisions in one of two ways: they observe that the state or judge is ultimately responsible for imposing the death sentence, or they employ such stories as a means for convincing a holdout. As Sherman Lewis, a white industrial plant manager from the Southeast, observed,

We talked to the holdout after the vote was down—it could have remained anonymous— but she spoke up and said, "I'm the one who voted against death." We did as the judge did, we reminded her what we were going to do was only give a recommendation. We told her that didn't mean that this was going to be what actually happened to him.

In an interesting variation on the conservative narrative of antijudicial activism,[7] the "only a recommendation" approach allows jurors simultaneously to deny responsibility for their sentencing decisions and to save face as jurors. "We did as the judge did" reveals how this narrative allows insiders to play the legal literalism card—"only a recommendation" enables them to defer to the power of the state.

The Tragedy of the Disadvantaged

The "tragedy of the disadvantaged" narrative enables jurors to rationalize any doubts about what defendants represent. The plot of this story, in effect, is "the defendant's life may be a tragedy, but he is still one of *them*." Deflecting a more explicit commitment to a tale of an inferior race, jurors' tragic stories enable them to articulate feelings of "failure or catastrophe as the ultimate end of the story" (Jacobs 2001, 224). Evoking tragedy thus enables jurors to create an alternative duality—juror as hero and defendant as villain:

> The revenge-tragedy is a simple tragic structure, and like most simple structures can be a very powerful one, often retained as a central theme even in the most complex tragedies. Here the original act provoking revenge sets up an antithetical or counterbalancing movement, and the completion of the movement resolves the tragedy. This happens so often that we may almost characterize the total mythos of tragedy as binary. (Frye 1957, 209)

The "tragedy of the disadvantaged" story is a fascinating variation on what has come to be known as compassionate conservatism. While the jurors in this book served on cases well before the presidency of George W. Bush, it becomes apparent how effective this discourse is for creating the appearance of being both sympathetic to the marginalized and tough on criminals. Especially when combined with other narratives such as a story of individual responsibility, jurors accomplish sympathy and represent the poor, black criminal. In the words of Avery Anderson, a white college-educated business executive, "It was a very sad situation all the way around. He was black, raised in the ghetto, and so on."

The Tale of an Inferior Race

This narrative often overlaps with the story of individual responsibility but is more explicitly about racial difference. While very few jurors employ explicitly racial epithets, others tell stories of black-on-black violence that imply a taken-for-granted understanding of violence as something to which blacks are more prone than whites. As Robert Waingrow, a white high-school-educated construction worker, put it, "I'm not going to be racial about it, but you have to state the facts: The blacks are killing the blacks."

The Bad Kid and the Caring Family

Calling the black or Hispanic defendant a bad kid enables whites to see themselves as disappointed or angry parents. This narrative is a paternalistic story drawn from common knowledge of irresponsible "bad" or "street" kids. It is evoked to belittle the defendant and thus to simplify the complexities of his life. As a white sales representative, Deidre Lund, responded,

> This kid got lost in system. Like a lost sheep, he had a pitiful background. He's basically a street kid. I'm not so sure he knows right from wrong like the rest of us.

Paternalism is also heard in the story of the caring family. As a kind of family, the jury must deal with members who deviate from the group. Focusing on convincing a nonwhite holdout to join the pro-death majority, whites tell stories of lending a sympathetic ear to the holdout's plight. They tell tales of coaxing the holdout back into the caring graces of the family. Compliance is typically reached by easing the holdout into confronting whether he or she is with or against the jury, for or against justice. As a white construction supervisor and jury foreman, Howard Lively, said,

> We had a very old black male with no education whatsoever. When it got down to sentencing, I found it very difficult, being the foreman of the jury. I didn't want to coax him into saying something he didn't feel like he needed to say, but I wanted him to understand why they were sentencing this guy to death. . . . He was very upset about saying yes to the death penalty. And I was afraid that when we went back out and the judge asked each one of us how we plead, he would say, "Not sure" or "No." So I told him, "When the judge talks to you,

just say, 'Yes sir.'" I don't want to say that we coached him into saying yes, but I guess in reality we did.

The Threatening Outsider

Relying on the only cultural capital they may possess—indeed, the only cultural capital that makes sense to them in the decision to take a life—jurors resort to telling tales of a threatening outsider. In this way, doing death is accomplished in explicit stories of racialized and/or gendered identities. Like the images represented in the Horton ads, jurors focus on the defendant's "dark," cold, or menacing appearance or hypermasculinity. However, threatening-outsider stories often defy simple categorizations of the defendant. In other words, these tales are windows into how jurors' construct identities as threatening and into how jurors respond to such threats through punishment. In response to the question "During the punishment phase, did any of the defense witnesses backfire?" Shirley Loman, a white secretary, stated,

His mother—really, his reaction to his mother's testimony. He was very unemotional through the whole trial, and when his mother got on the stand and pleaded for his life, he didn't bat an eye, not a tear, no emotion at all. That pretty much put him in the electric chair.

Jurors' Stories as Hegemonic Tales

The hegemonic is not simply a static body of ideas to which members of a culture are obliged to conform. [It] has a protean nature in which dominant relations are preserved while their manifestations remain highly flexible. The hegemonic must continually evolve so as to recuperate alternative hegemonies.

—Sandra Silberstein, "Ideology as Process" (1988)

Narratives depict understandings of particular persons and events, they reproduce, without exposing, the connections of the specific story and persons to the structure of relations and institutions that made the story plausible.

—Patricia Ewick and Susan S. Silbey,
"Subversive Stories and Hegemonic Tales" (1995)

Capital jurors' multiple, often conflicting narratives mask a meta-narrative—a hegemonic tale of moral insiders and immoral outsiders. Consequently, how jurors do death is simultaneously how they do dominant-subordinate relations. Instantiating a broader antiequality hegemonic through the telling, combining, retelling, and recombining of these tales, jurors' decisions are polyvocal articulations at the same time that they are remarkably normative in character. In this way, punishment as a hegemonic accomplishment is taken for granted, bound up in the identities of those who punish. It is muffled in the many voices that normalize domination as penal action.

The identity-hegemony nexus elucidates the contours of jurors' death penalty consciousness. Disciplined by dominant hegemonies, capital jurors in effect reenact a politics of the insiders as punishment. Thus, punishing the criminal in the late twentieth century also entails silencing any voices of resistance. Both the immoral outsider and the resister are, to obviously very different degrees, simultaneously punished under law.

Subverting Death

The complex ideological web that insiders weave leaves little room for resistance; holdouts bear the ominous burden of empowering themselves against the will of a punitive majority. Yet the experiences of actually making the life-or-death decision may mobilize potent voices of resistance. Successfully integrating identities of resistance into their role as jurors, resisters successfully turn the tide against the insiders. Jurors who have unique experiences that help them relate to defendants or that help them to see weaknesses in insiders' narratives serve as fascinating case studies. I explore resisters' stories in chapter 5. In the next chapter, I turn to a more detailed analysis of the stories of the insiders.

Chapter 4
Insiders

Sheila Brooks: "He Wasn't a White Kid"

Sheila Brooks, a white college-educated hairdresser and mother of two, served on a capital jury that sentenced to death Ray Floyd Cornish, a black male convicted of shooting a white male convenience store clerk. This was her first time serving on a jury.

Sheila Brooks told the interviewer that imposing the death sentence "was a very hard decision." While she believes that the jury made the right choice on punishment, she would prefer not to serve on a capital case again. In the course of her three-hour interview, she did not offer many stories—most of her answers were short and to the point. However, she was quite forthcoming when the interviewer asked, "During the trial, what were your impressions of the defendant?"

> I saw the defendant as a very typical product of the lower socioeconomic black group who grew up with no values, no ideals, no authority, no morals, no leadership, and this has come down from generation to generation. And that was one of the problems we had, for me, and in the jury. Because some of the jurors were looking at him as your average white kid: he wasn't a white kid. He came from a totally different environment. I'm just saying that he was the one that was the defendant. And I just saw him as a loser from day one, as soon as he was born into that environment, and into that set of people who basically were into drugs, alcohol, illegitimacy, AIDS, the whole nine yards. This kid didn't have a chance. That's how I saw the defendant. And there are ten thousand others like him out there, which is very tragic.

Sheila Brooks's "tragedy of the black group" tale conveys what might best be called a white racial dialectic. Labeling the defendant as part of a valueless black group, she simultaneously reinforces her own superior white identity. Comparing her view to that of her counterparts on the jury, Sheila informs them that "he wasn't a white kid." Moreover, her use of ambiguous adjectives and phrases such as "that," "totally different," "that set of people," and the "whole nine yards" reveals a broader and more pervasive ideological means for distancing herself from a defendant she sees as lacking in individuality. Indeed, she sees him as part of a subordinate black subculture. Nevertheless, she observes, "there are ten thousand others like him out there, which is very tragic." The defendant is thus just another character in her story. For Sheila Brooks, Cornish's black life fits a tragedy that is all too familiar.

In this story, Cornish's life is part of a tragic story that blacks don't have a chance at the same time that they are pitiful losers. Having difficulty relating to a defendant "born into *that* environment," Sheila Brooks's story marks entire places as breeding grounds for black inferiority, as drug-ridden, AIDS-infested places; places far away (albeit, tragically) from where "average white kids" live. Next, when asked, "In your mind, how well do the following words describe the defendant: 'Severely abused as a child,'" she responds,

> I believe that was what he endured most as a child: severe neglect. They were from the lower socioeconomic black group. From what we read about in the paper a lot, he was definitely from that group.

The popular media, as Antonio Gramsci classically observes, is a key transmitter of hegemony. For Sheila Brooks, media confirms that "black" is more than just a category for designating the defendant Cornish—it is also a story of what "these people are." She then provides an individual-responsibility story of her husband's struggles with addiction into her broader cultural-distance narrative.

I did think about my first husband, who was a drug addict, and that's how I know what a drug addict is. And they didn't prove that to me. And drug addicts don't go out and kill people.

The final sentence serves as an important hegemonic end in Sheila Brooks's story. By using the story of her husband's addiction as a matrix for understanding the defendant's addiction, she sees Cornish as culturally remote—she confirms what she already knows about drug addicts. At the same time, the story of her husband allows her to come across as color-blind or race neutral. Because "drug addicts don't go out and kill people," she rationalizes the complexities of Cornish's problems with illicit drugs. In contrast to her earlier story of the "lower socioeconomic black group," comparing the defendant's and her husband's addictions allows her to seamlessly transition to an evaluation of Cornish's culpability for murder.

Employing episodes from their private lives, white jurors tell stories that are inconsistent and often contradictory explanations for how they came to know the defendant. Such inconsistencies and contradictions help to explain how the racial-inferiority narrative is a taken-for-granted part of doing death on the racially defined Other. Unlike the subordinate racial group, white jurors need not be consistent. They need only to confirm what they already believe—that the defendant is everything or anything that they are not (black and addicted).

Melvin Seagal: "I Call Them Lost Souls"

Stories of personal experiences lend an air of authority to jurors' stories. According to Melvin Seagal, a retired white social worker who sat in judgment of Frank Sharpe, an African American male convicted of shooting to death his uncle,

I lived in New York City for seventeen years, and I saw a lot of youngsters like [Sharpe] in the ghettos up there, who were just lost souls. I call them lost souls. They have the propensity to do great harm to others because they have a lot of rage. They have a lot of unresolved anger. So, yes, I've seen young men and women who very much reminded me of him. They're powder kegs, they're just—their emotions are just simmering beneath the surface. And that's where I was exposed to a lot of people like him, when I was living in New York City.

Comparing his experiences working with ghetto youngsters with Sharpe's experiences bolsters the veracity of Melvin Seagal's story. By contrast to Sheila Brooks's explicitly lay, nonexpert tale of a "lower socioeconomic black group," Melvin Seagal employs his identity as an experienced insider. Yet Seagal's story conveys essentially the same plot as Brooks's: blacks such as Frank Sharpe are "lost souls," "they have the propensity to do great harm," "they have a lot of rage." Drawing on his experiences with marginalized African American youths, Seagal represents himself as an expert testifying to the defendant's outsider identity. By adding the story of "ghetto lost souls" into his evaluation of the defendant, Seagal implicitly avoids evaluating Frank Sharpe's marginality.

Albert Reynolds: "I Took Charge. . . . There's Only One Reason You Pull Out a Gun"

Stories of personal experience express both empathy for the defendant's circumstances and confirmation of his responsibility for murder. Albert Reynolds is a white high-school-educated mechanic and Vietnam veteran. Reynolds served on a jury that sentenced to death Barry Lawrence, a white man caught on videotape robbing and shooting to death a Hispanic convenience store clerk. Responding to a question about the defendant's upbringing, Reynolds tells a fascinating tale about his troubled youth, his final reckoning with the criminal justice system, and his eventual transformation in the U.S. Navy.

The judge said, "You either go in the service, or you go to jail." I ended up in the navy. My mother went before the judge that had me on probation and said that I didn't realize what I was doing. So I went into the service in February of 1965. That definitely changed me. I mean, I did brig time in the navy—I got thrown into the brig for fighting. For thirty days I was in the brig, and I said, "I just can't go on like this." I mean, when I got out that time, I said to myself, "Time to buckle down!" I really wanted to do better. I wanted to show my parents I could do something better in my life. Lawrence was also in and out of trouble. I felt sorry for him. I just wondered why a person would keep letting his life go on like that. Why didn't he just do it? I mean, you go where you have to. I took charge. I didn't let anybody control my life.

Embedding his own fascinating story of personal redemption into his evaluation of the defendant, Albert Reynolds struggles to understand why Barry Lawrence failed to "take charge." But what is striking in Reynolds's story is the absence of any detail surrounding Lawrence's life history. While the jury was informed during the punishment phase that Lawrence, unlike Reynolds, had been abandoned by his family at an early age and had never had a parental figure in his life, Albert Reynolds never discusses these critical differences between his life history and that of the defendant. Lawrence's story is, in the end, one of tragedy. Reynolds "feels sorry" for Lawrence but fails to recognize that the defendant's life has lacked the privilege that Reynolds possesses. Indeed, when asked to reflect on what convinced him of the defendant's guilt, Reynolds observes,

The videotape was very powerful. I own a handgun, and to me, there's only one reason you pull out a handgun, and that's because you're gonna use it. Just the thought of him pulling out a handgun and deliberately shooting another person! It irritates the heck out of me! Even after Vietnam and everything else. I just can't really describe it.

As both a gun owner and a Vietnam veteran, Albert Reynolds is at a loss to understand Barry Lawrence's act of senseless violence, caught vividly on videotape. Despite the defense's story of Lawrence's emotionally abusive childhood, Reynolds is unable to step outside the box of his own life. Albert Reynolds's autobiography serves only to reinforce his identity as an insider and the defendant's identity as immoral outsider.

From Racial Tragedy to Racial Contempt

Media and jurors' personal resources give meaning to an underlying clash of cultures in jurors' cultural-distance stories. Both popular culture and personal experiences help jurors confirm what they already know about blacks such as the defendant. Using such cultural and personal capital enables jurors to see the defendant as Other and, indeed, worthy of the death sentence.

"Death worthiness" in juirors' stories may also be told through the prism of the defendant's crime. In this way, jurors combine an emotionally charged tale of black violence with their reactions to the murder. Unlike the previous examples, the tragedy of the black group tale gives way to a story of contempt for the defendant and what he represents that constitutes part of a broader epidemic that must be avenged.

Robert Waingrow: "And You Don't Do It Gently"

Robert Waingrow, a white high-school-educated construction worker, served on a case involving Ivan Strayhorn, a black man who murdered his stepmother. Waingrow begins by telling the tragically familiar story about how "the blacks are killing the blacks." Here, Waingrow offers his reactions to the murder of Strayhorn's mother:

> It's a shame—a woman that lived a good life, you know? And it's just a shame to see the way she went. I'm not going to be racial about it, but you have to state the facts: The blacks are killing the blacks. And you don't do it gently. It's just brutal. You think that he would do that to somebody who put her hand out to help him?

Robert Waingrow's story of escalating black-on-black violence is a matrix for understanding Strayhorn's responsibility for the crime. Indeed, it helps the juror to make sense of the defendant's sense-lessness. "I'm not going to be racial about it" is Waingrow's attempt to distance himself from the defendant, but it may also be interpreted as relevant for understanding the sentencing decision. Jurors such as Robert Waingrow voice sympathy for disadvantaged blacks more broadly but do not "do it gently."

> I thought death was even too good. . . . It should be a slow death, as a matter of fact. Bring back the old Nazi piano wire. That's pretty bad, but we all agreed. This other juror and I, he was in Korea. We both agreed just give him to us. Give me an hour with him. It was just unbelievable! You wouldn't do it to a dog, to an animal. He had no remorse. The kid had no remorse. He didn't feel any shame. Then he had the nerve at the end to say that he was sorry! That he didn't mean to kill his stepmother: Get outta here! He left her down there for three and a half days. He didn't mean to kill her!?! What the hell were you gonna do to her? He didn't give her anything to drink, nothing to eat, zero.

Pausing briefly, Robert Waingrow attempts to distance himself from his earlier story of the "blacks are killing the blacks."

> It had nothing to do with his race, the fact that he was black. We didn't even look at him that way.

Beginning with the first part of his story, Robert Waingrow's vengeance story is accomplished through racially coded phrases such as "no remorse" and "no shame." The paternalistic story of the bad kid is also important for understanding Waingrow's impressions of Strayhorn as immature and as someone not to be taken seriously. Moreover, focusing on the defendant's violence, Waingrow makes no reference to the detailed information of Strayhorn's troubled childhood presented during the trial. Instead, the juror relies on an implicit story of individual responsibility that distances him from the more complex matters concerning the tragedy of the disadvantaged.

Robert Waingrow demonstrates how critical race is in his story. Referring to the color line, his story employs a racialized discourse that creates the facade of a death-sentencing decision based solely on the defendant's conduct. In this way, Waingrow can be interpreted here as trying to downplay his wanting to use "the old Nazi piano wire" on this "kid" he described in the first part of his vengeance story.

Drawing on the media, Robert Waingrow expresses moral indignation at what he sees as an epidemic of outsider immorality, an epidemic that is spreading into the white middle-class community.

> If they did it once, they'll do it again. I'm fairly convinced that they have no conscience. It's being done every day of the week here. Just turn the news on—we got kids killing kids. It's out of control! These kids are thirteen years old!
>
> And they are all white, wealthy kids! They're not poor kids. They beat people to death with a baseball bat? Get outta here! I believe if they do it once, they'll do it again. To take a life, you can't bring them back.

What is fascinating about Waingrow's broken justice story is his conscious need to call attention to the growing number of youthful predators as now a white middle-class problem. Thus, his story tacitly relies on the tale of racial inferiority. It reveals a racialized set of expectations—that wealthy whites are not typically violent.

Nevertheless, his story of who is and is not violent obviously depends on racial knowledge. His argument, "You can't bring them back," because these kids "are wealthy and white," reveals a clearly racialized (and ageist) perspective on violence. Put another way, Waingrow's story can be interpreted as saying, "If they had been poor and black, then such violence would not be surprising."

Ralph Lewis: "Every Time . . . I Meet a Nigger"

Older, less-educated white jurors' stories convey an even more explicit contempt for blacks. Such jurors weave racial epithets into their stories; they explicitly see blacks as inferior. Marking the defendant with a racial identity rooted in a hopeless and savagely violent black group, they express an utter lack of surprise about the defendant's actions.

Ralph Lewis is a white retired farmer born and raised in Alabama and is, in a word, proud of his southern background. Throughout his interview, he seemed to take great pride in the thickness of his accent. While there were some audio problems and thus some difficulties in transcribing his three-hour interview, Lewis's description of Alfred Watson, a black man convicted of shooting a black victim, apparently in a failed drug deal, was captured by the tape recorder.

> Anybody that was born and raised in the South when I was born and raised in the South and says they're not prejudiced is a liar. I try very, very hard to get over it. Every time . . . I meet a nigger, and I don't like white ones any more than I do black ones. That's the way it is. And what difference [there is] between me and anybody else is that I admit it. . . . I mean, like when I heard about the killing, I thought, "Well, they're just wiping each other out again." You know, if they'd been white people, I would've had a different attitude.

Ralph Lewis's overt racism obviously elucidates his underlying contempt for African Americans such as Alfred Watson. While only one other juror in the sample referred to a defendant as a "nigger," such contempt stories, albeit more explicitly than Robert Waingrow's story, convey a very similar point: this defendant's violence is indicative of a racially inferior group. However, "They're just wiping each other out again" and "If they'd been white people, I would've had a different attitude" are more than just obvious racist blather. Viewed through the lens of punishment at the hands of the state, Lewis's story reveals how sentencing the Other has as much to do with constructing black identities as with confirming whiteness.

When Blacks Hold Out for Life

The story of the caring family is a matrix for how the white majority can convince a black holdout to impose the death sentence. Describing the holdout's reluctance to impose the death sentence because of his or her identification with the defendant's race or, more generally, mistrust of the criminal justice system, jurors in the majority tell stories of a sympathetic attempt to understand the fellow juror's differences with the group.

Rather than resorting to outright intimidation of the minority, white male jurors tell a story of the "caring father," an almost cordial approach, to convince the nonwhite holdout. As Mary R. Jackman observes,

> Within these constraints, the dominant group relies more on love or reasoning as instruments of coercion than on hostility and force. These efforts do not fall into a void, but set the moral parameters of the dialogue with the subordinates. If the structure of the relationship is conducive, subordinates may be trapped into generous compliance. (1996, 74)

White males tell stories that show their attempt to understand or at least acknowledge the subordinate's point of view. What distinguishes such attempts, however, is how paternalism becomes an especially effective discourse—a means for trapping the holdout by the serenade into "generous compliance."

Fred Dawson: "The Fact That It Is One of Your Brothers"

Fred Dawson, a white business executive, served on the case of Devon Wiggins, a black male who shot to death a white grocery store clerk.[1] The jury was made up of eleven whites (six females

and five males) and one black woman. At the sentencing phase, all
of the jurors except for the African American woman had made up
their minds that Wiggins deserved death. Here, Dawson tells how
the jury persuaded her to join the majority.

> The only disagreement was with the black lady. She was a
> bright, a very nice lady. She had problems before—her son
> had been picked up, accused of a crime falsely, because he
> was black. She was a little bit sour on the system, but he got
> out of it. They found the other two black kids. So we were
> talking about that, and she looked across the table and she
> said, "I was the one who voted for life, you know?" I said,
> "You don't have to tell me that." I said, "But I know you
> were having trouble, the fact that it is one of your brothers."
> And she said, "He really ain't no brother of mine. He's a bad
> dude, bad." So I said, "Well, that's up to you." She said,
> "Why don't we vote again?" And it was twelve to zero. And
> then she sat there and cried for twenty minutes. But she was a
> good lady.

Dawson's story of the caring father immediately draws attention to
the "very nice," "bright," "black lady." Conveying a sense of sympathy, Dawson then quickly shifts to a story of what made her different from the rest of the jurors (us). Dawson is, indeed, careful to
acknowledge the validity of the African American holdout's mistrust of a criminal justice system that "falsely accused" her son of
a crime. Furthermore, his introduction creates a sense of rising
curiosity in the reader; the focus now is almost completely on the
"good black lady."

Dawson's story is also a tragic one. Speaking in her voice, he
sounds both sympathetic to and understanding of her "black
plight." However, not until Dawson recounts her response to the
challenge of "having to sentence one of your brothers," is the utility of paternalism as a device for achieving compliance revealed.
Dawson simultaneously expresses sympathy for the black juror's
predicament and turns the tables on her. Employing a dominance

of care, he coaxes her into confronting what he perceives as her own black protectionism. But Dawson is careful to represent himself as a caring and sympathetic father figure ("Well, that's up to you"). Care and sympathy allow him to avoid the implications of the obviously racial tactics he has used to make the black holdout see things his way. Paternalism, especially in the context of the give-and-take of deliberations, is perhaps the most effective and indeed subtle discourse for creating the illusion of a color-blind and sympathetic decision-making process.

While paternalism and sympathy played a role in the jury's deliberations, Dawson was anything but sympathetic toward the defendant and what he represents.

> INTERVIEWER: Did you have the following thoughts or feelings about the defendant? You felt anger or rage toward him.
>
> FRED DAWSON: I was angry because hundreds of thousands of people are like this throughout the country who cause all this aggravation and money to be spent on the court system. It's just ridiculous! It's wasting my time.
>
> INTERVIEWER: Did you feel contempt or hatred for the defendant's family?
>
> FRED DAWSON: I don't hate anyone. It's the same bullshit that never stops. There's too much of it. Our welfare system makes these people—our dollars we give them. It's terrible and awful.
>
> INTERVIEWER: In your mind, how well do the following words describe the killing? It made you sick to think about it.
>
> FRED DAWSON: No, because that is a personal thing. I don't get upset about people like that. I just want to put him away from society. Hang them if they have to be hung, or the death penalty, whatever. I am sick and tired of this. It's a fairly universal attitude of people today. There is so much stupid crime! It's ridiculous, you know? We have so many liberal "do-wells"—those bleeding-heart liberals. This is nonsense. The guy knew what he was doing when he pumped four shots into the guy.

The nexus of white middle-class male identity and conservative, tough-on-crime rhetoric is audible in each of Fred Dawson's responses. Replete with racially coded phrases such as "these" people and "the same bullshit that never stops," his angry responses stem not only from the defendant's actions but also from whom Wiggins and his family represent. Thus, Dawson's individual-responsibility story has little to do with an individualized assessment of the defendant's conduct. Rather, Dawson's identity is one of a conservative avenger—he sees himself as evening the score against the pro-welfare, liberal establishment he blames for producing "the Devon Wigginses of America"—a racialized discourse heavily employed during the Reagan and George H. W. Bush presidencies (Omi and Winant 1994).

Fred Dawson focuses his contempt for Wiggins's crime on the liberal "do-wells." In effect, he reconciles the contradiction in the Cornish trial juror Sheila Brooks's assessment of the defendant as both responsible for his actions and a product of his tragic black environment. In Dawson's story, antiliberal rhetoric is a justification in and of itself—it is taken for granted as the way things are ("a fairly universal attitude"). And it enables Dawson to make Wiggins's crime personal ("our dollars we give them") at the same time that it obscures Dawson's racist stereotypes of a dangerous black welfare class.

Bernadette Garvin: "A Pretty Typical Situation"

In other instances, the "caring family" can fracture into a tale of a jury divided. While this rarely happens across racial lines, as blacks are nearly always a very small minority in death cases (Bowers, Sandys, and Steiner 2001), the jury may break apart across gendered lines, particularly when the victim's identity threatens heterosexual male jurors. Bernadette Garvin, a white college-educated homemaker sentenced to life without parole Lawrence Kendrick, a white man convicted of using a hammer to beat to death a homosexual man with AIDS, Thomas Winter, in an apparent hate-related crime.

During deliberations, we had a whole gamut of things come out about sex, homosexuals, how men feel about homosexuals, and how women feel about homosexuals. That was one of the major things that happened. We could have gone in there if the man had not been a homosexual and got it done. It would have been a much easier decision. But the minute homosexuality came in, and the fact that the man had AIDS came in, all the men went to this side and all the women went to other. It was a pretty typical situation. . . . The men just couldn't understand that a murder is a murder regardless of whether or not the victim is gay and has AIDS.

Bernadette Garvin finds "typical" the heterosexual male jurors' revulsion toward the AIDS-infected gay victim. Homophobia, late-twentieth-century-style, makes its way into jury decision making and has consequences for how state law is enforced. Separating themselves from the more sympathetic female jurors, the heterosexual male jurors' behavior is expressly political. To them, the victim is worth inherently less than a "normal," noninfected heterosexual. Deciding the fate of a gay victim in death cases in a historical period of growing homophobia,[2] capital jurors like many in the current judiciary send

a message that the courts inten[d] to be vigilant in controlling the spread of the epidemic to the mainstream of America, consistent with historical responses of the courts to enable repression of already stigmatized populations as an effective symbolic response to lethal epidemics. (Drass, Gregware, and Musheno 1997, 295)

For the male jurors, people with AIDS are inherently less human and make the decision to impose the death sentence difficult. Bernadette Garvin's description of the jury's decision as "not easy" elucidates how morality and identity, including sexual orientation, combine in the jury's decision to impose punishment.

Angela Stephens: "The Defendant Is a White Man and the Victim Was a Black Man. [The Juror] Was a Pathetic Human Being"

The rare instance of a white defendant facing the death penalty for murdering a black victim creates chaos in the jury room. The white holdout refuses to impose the death sentence and fractures the caring family.

> He announced he would allow us to speak to him if we could speak in unemotional tones, and, if we so chose, we could try to convince him that he was wrong and we were right. And he would not guarantee that he could change his mind, but he was willing to listen. So three hours later, when we were about to come to blows, he announced that there was no way he was going to vote for the death penalty. That he only believed in the death penalty in the case of mass murderers, people like Adolf Hitler and Jeffrey Dahmer. Then he mentioned one black man who was in jail for killing a white woman, that he could have given him the death penalty. So we pretty much knew what we were dealing with. We were dealing with a racist. And we were dealing with someone who had lied about the death penalty during jury selection that he could vote for it. He lied when the prosecutor asked him, "Do you realize the defendant is a white man and the victim was a black man? Would that change any weight in your deliberations?" And he said, "Absolutely not." He was a pathetic human being.

Angela Stephens, a white college-educated sales manager, tells a fascinating and complex story of a holdout she perceives as a racist fraud. Her story is a powerful, tension-filled tale of twelve angry jurors. Rejecting the holdout's story of an inferior race, she describes the jury as parajudging, or making a judgment within a judgment, in which this juror's credibility is now on trial. Indeed, as she describes the "verdict": "We pretty much knew what we were dealing with." Finally, closing with the story of the "pathetic human being" who lied during jury selection, she elucidates how white defendant–black victim cases may be inescapably volatile. Indeed, given that blacks continue to be racialized as dangerous criminals and whites as innocent victims,[3] jury decision making may turn into outright racial conflict.

The Threatening Outsider

Threatening-outsider stories focus on the defendant's appearance or behavior in court, employ popular images of the defendant as evil or immature, or confirm that the defendant is attempting to manipulate the jury. Jurors offer straightforward descriptions of defendants' appearance or demeanor in the courtroom; jurors get a handle on with whom they are dealing. Two jurors gave the following responses when asked to comment on defendants' appearances during trials.

> RALPH LEWIS: I thought he was just a little bit arrogant, maybe even pompous. When we were chosen, he'd lean back, enjoying the hour. It kind of irked me. (Watson case)
> ANGELA STEPHENS: Arrogant—you would think he'd throw himself on the mercy of the jury and try to look remorseful. (Bishop case)

Other jurors comment on defendants' lack of emotion or remorselessness during the punishment phase.

> TERRY JANSEN: The hardest part was just watching him sit there and not show any feelings at all. (Suarez case)
> STUART BRAND: He showed so little emotion and so little remorse. We just wanted to kind of figure out, "Are you human!?!" (Suarez case)
> ANGELA STEPHENS: He was over there just looking like it was another day at the office. No remorse whatsoever. No remorse, no apologies. (Bishop case)

Describing defendants in court, jurors offer broader expectations of how the Other behaves. Some jurors reflect on their own behavior as if they were in the defendants' position.

> PAMELA DRAKE: The guy showed no remorse. I couldn't believe it. I'd be sweating it out if I was gonna get killed or go to jail for half my life. (Raymond case)

Imagining the Threatening Outsider

Jurors tell stories of a threatening Other; they imagine the defendant as evil. They express disbelief at the defendant's lack of emotion. They mobilize the law's romantic narrative of good triumphing over evil. Seeing the defendant as solely evil and the law as solely good powerfully simplifies their task and thus enables them to know. In this way, romance, as Northrop Frye observed,

> follows its general dialectic structure, which means that subtlety and complexity are not much favored. Characters tend to either be for or against the quest. If they assist it they are idealized as simply gallant and pure; if they obstruct it they are caricatured as simply villainous or cowardly. Hence every typical character in romance tends to have his moral opposite confronting him, like black and white pieces in a chess game. (1957, 194)

> LEANNE CROFT: If he had just turned around to the jury and said, "I didn't mean to do it." Or, "I'm sorry I did it. . . . It was dumb to do it." Or something, you know—just something, you would have had compassion for this person. But they sit there, and they say absolutely nothing! I don't care if they get torn up on the stand by the prosecuting attorney! At least say a few words to the stands when it's a capital offense! I mean, there are twelve people that are going to decide the rest of your life. For God's sake, say a few words to them! I mean, that's how I feel about it. (Paxton case)

"They say absolutely nothing" confirms this juror's predetermined expectations about the defendant's immorality or evil; the outsiders outrage Leanne Croft. Raising an impassioned plea for black defendant Cyrus Paxton to demonstrate his humanity, Croft builds an obvious climactic tension in her story. But when the threatening outsider has been constructed as the evil villain, she employs her own anguish ("At least say a few words!"), which, in turn, marks Paxton and those like him as innately villainous (see Katz 1998). Thus, the story of the evil villain explicitly enables Leanne Croft to dehumanize Paxton.

Jurors' stories of the threatening outsider mobilize other narratives, such as the paternalistic story of the bad kid.

> FRANK DOD: The defendant didn't show any remorse for what he'd done. It was almost like trying a kid for breaking a lamp. You have the child, and you have the broken lamp. Perhaps there are some bruises on the child's hand where he tried to pick it up or what have you. But he didn't realize that maybe he'd broken an expensive lamp and probably didn't care. He'd probably knock another one over. That's what he was like. (Watson case)

Other jurors do not mince words when describing the defendant.

> FRANK DOD: He's a beast. (Watson case)
> ANNE HERNANDEZ: He was an evil person. (Wallace case)
> JESSIE SALVI: He's a sociopath. (Wallace case)
> STUART BRAND: He made me think of Charles Manson. (Suarez case)

Confirming Threat

Seeing the defendant behave as the immoral Other powerfully confirms jurors' ideology as insiders. Focusing on how defendants looked at members of the jury, jurors paint an image of a gawking predator. Similar to what Angela Davis (1978) has described in her critique of the mythical hypersexualized black male rapist of white women, jurors describe defendants as threatening brutes who are more concerned with satisfying their lustful urges than with whether they live or die.

> MARY ALBANY: There was one beautiful girl who was an alternate juror but did not get chosen for the jury. At the close of the trial, she had to go out to the courtroom and sit before we went back to deliberation, and he eyed her the whole time. He turned all the way around in his seat to watch her go to her seat and sit down. Everyone noticed that. He was real confident for someone facing the death penalty. (Bishop case)

Alternatively, jurors describe defendants as possessing an "I don't care," almost boastful, attitude.

> MARY ALBANY: After seeing the photographs of the victim and hearing the evidence and seeing the expression on his face. That "I don't care" attitude—"So I did it. So what?" (Bishop case)

Jurors tell stories of the threatening outsider trying to directly deceive or manipulate them. Focusing on various courtroom scenes, jurors see through what they perceive as defendants' transparent attempts to curry favor.

> RALPH LEWIS: He read his little statement they had given him. He just didn't sound like that was anything at all he wanted to say. He was apologizing to the family and saying he was sorry, but he didn't even do a good job of it. Acting isn't his strong suit. (Watson case)

Others see defendants' family members as selfishly trying to play on the jury's sympathy.

FLORENCE DELBERT: His mother screamed. She stood up and screamed, got hysterical. She screamed, "Don't kill my baby!" And I was offended. . . . Her baby just murdered somebody and had been found guilty of that. I don't think it's her fault that he did what he did, 'cause he was a big boy and he's responsible for his actions. But for her to scream, "Don't kill my baby!" when her baby had just killed somebody else's baby wasn't fair. I mean, it wasn't fair to us, and it certainly wasn't fair to [the victim's] parents and anybody that cared about her. (Elisé case)

Florence Delbert views the mother's emotional plea as an affront to the jury's integrity, as a way to bamboozle the jurors into sparing her son's life. Alternatively, manipulation can be combined with racial inferiority. For example, a non-English-speaking defendant's testimony through a translator is seen as a thinly veiled attempt to manipulate.

WALTER ROBERTSON: I remember right when they were getting ready to, you know, take the stand, the prosecutor was kinda leading him into—he got him right where he wanted him. . . . And then he started speaking in Spanish instead of English, and we'd have to go to an interpreter. We knew he could speak English well enough. He was just trying to make more of a hassle or something. (Rodriguez case)

Others focus on what they perceive as defendants' doctored appearances, describing defendants as "all dressed up" to manipulate the jurors into believing that alleged criminals are somehow "normal," All-American boys.

DOROTHY ANTONIO: He looked nice, like an All-American boy. I'll tell you one thing, that doesn't sway my opinion. Take a person who looks grungy and stubbly and clean him up and shave him and put a suit on him. That cannot affect me. It's the way a person looks themselves, when you look

them in the eye. That gets me. That makes a difference.
(Bishop case)

Overview of Chapter 4

Jurors' stories overwhelmingly reveal how popular and personal constructions of the immoral outsider insidiously guide those given the responsibility to make life-or-death sentencing decisions. Jurors' story worlds of death enable them to make sense out of their decisions to sentence to death the Othered: These interconnecting morality narratives illuminate both the jurors' identities as punishers and how they construct or reconstruct the punished.

Incorporating stories from personal experience and popular culture, capital jurors tell tales "that reveal far more commonalities than unique characteristics" (van Dijk 1993, 141). Insiders' stories reveal death penalty judgments to be a potent practice for clarifying dominant moralities. Confronting both their own and defendants' identities, jurors' stories of their death-sentencing decisions are as much about moral culpability and just desserts as about mobilizing dominant and confirming subordinate identities. As Trish Oberweis and Michael Musheno cogently observe,

> Moral decisions themselves are acts of identification, each decision—and the legitimation for that decision—subtly informing social relations between actors. Such social relations are always already tainted by the traces of power, with some actors assuming more power than others in any given interaction. (2001, 65)

Chapter 5
Voices of Resistance

You don't want smart people. Now, I wish that you could ask everyone's IQ, you could pick a great jury all the time. You don't want smart people.

—Former Philadelphia District Attorney Jack McMahon (1986)

The state ensures that those who do death are insiders; prosecutors seek jurors who believe that the death penalty is needed to combat "immoral outsiders" and all they represent. Prosecuting officials seek, in effect, to cleanse the capital jury of resisters. Ever weary of those who are more likely to question state authority, prosecutors are well rehearsed in covertly employing the tactics of exclusion. Prosecutors are trained to seek out the "best" (insiders) and the "worst" (resisters) jurors. As "The McMahon Tape,"[1] a jury-selection training tape for prosecutors, elucidates,

> The best jurors are stable, conservative, well dressed people from good neighborhoods, who are not particularly bright, and who are not inclined to analyze critically the government's case . . . a panel of middle class jurors of comparable intellectual ability, a group characteristic that facilitates consensus building. The worst jurors according to McMahon are "blacks from the low-income areas," because they are less likely to convict as a result of "resentment for law enforcement [and] for authority." (Baldus et al. 2001, 43)

The selection of the jury is not a perfect science, and "bad" capital jurors sometimes, although rarely, slip through the cracks. Such jurors mobilize narratives of resistance. As resisters, they tell stories of white middle-class indifference to a marginalized defendant's life, stories that resist the decision to impose the death sentence as "only a recommendation." Resisters tell stories of personal experiences that produce feelings of empathy for defendants that resisters struggle to communicate to insiders.

African American working-class resisters offer passionate voices infused with a racial consciousness reminiscent of black civil-rights-era activists (Morris 1986). Alternatively, more educated black resisters attempt to inform their white counterparts of the various socioeconomic challenges faced by marginalized communities of color. While black working-class resisters angrily condemn their white counterparts as individual racists, better-educated black resisters tend to be more sensitive to what they describe as the pervasive effects of racial segregation on distorted white expectations of African American life.

Ronald Fredrickson: "They Wanted to Fry Those Black Boys"

Working-class black males, including Ronald Fredrickson, voice strong resistance against their white counterparts on juries. Fredrickson, an auto mechanic, served on the case of Arthur Chester, a black man convicted of murdering a white police officer. When asked, "In your own words, can you tell me what the jury did to reach its decision about the defendant's punishment?" Fredrickson responded,

> They wanted to fry those black boys. I'm serious, that's the feeling I got. I felt that they didn't give a shit one way or the other. They wanted to go home to their husbands or to the football game instead of worrying about whether these people were going to die or not. They felt like, "These two black boys took a white man's life: We're going to burn them." That's the impression I got from a lot of the jurors. . . . I really believe they wanted to burn both of those guys because they were black and because the white defendant had a plea bargain and we didn't even hear his testimony. He was there just as much as the other black guy was.

Fredrickson's story reveals a deep alienation and hostility toward the white majority. He expresses resistance to the pervasive white hegemonic of black inferiority, of which he is acutely aware. The phrase "to their husbands" is perhaps the clearest example of his resistance to a system he views as privileging whites. His use of the generalized descriptive "their" suggests a more global perspective of the struggle for racial justice as well. Moreover, "football games"—as a trope for white indifference—both articulates to the interviewer the white majority's lack of concern for Chester's life and suggests a critique of the privileged white suburban lifestyle. Fredrickson, a working-class high-school-educated man, employs a racialized discourse of a society deeply polarized by race and class inequality.

Although Ronald Fredrickson never joined the pro-death majority—he was outvoted in an eventual majority-rule decision for death—his last two sentences here highlight his awareness of racial inequity in the criminal justice system ("He was there just as much"). Yet Fredrickson's story reveals more than a diffuse mistrust of the criminal justice system. Such a broad belief in the context of the Chester case can be heard as galvanizing Fredrickson's internal resistance to people such as Ralph Lewis who believe that blacks are an inferior race.

Harold Brown: "Totally Different Perspective of What Happens in the Inner City"

Some African American jurors share familiar experiences with whites. These stories confirm why blacks resist white racism. Another black juror, Harold Brown, a high-school-educated carpenter, explained how the jury made its decision to sentence to death Dwayne Whitmore, an African American convicted of killing another African American in an apparent gang-related dispute.

> People got their opinion before the trial actually started. Like this guy from up north. He had a totally different perspective of what happens in the inner city compared to the guy out in the suburbs who thinks, "If it's a black thing then its auto-

matic guilty." The white woman on the jury says the same thing. The white woman from west city who gets on the elevator with me, she got a problem. If something went down, the first thing that's gonna come out of her mouth, "It was a black guy." It's an automatic thing. And it's a shame to think that way when these white jurors hooked up that they were so disinterested. They were more concerned about what we were gonna have for lunch, and how long was lunch, and when we're gonna get out of there.

As with Ronald Fredrickson, Harold Brown's story can be heard as revealing a powerful sense of resistance against the racially biased white jurors. He embeds a story from outside the jury room into his broader narrative about resisting white racism. In this way, the hypothetical elevator episode serves not only to highlight racial bias among white jurors but also to convey it as taken for granted. In other words, Brown's story can be interpreted as saying, "If whites are racists in elevators, then they obviously also will be racists when deciding whether to sentence a black defendant to death."

Shirley Sharpe: "I Felt Like an Outsider"

Shirley Sharpe, a college-educated secretary, tells a more sympathetic story of culturally distant whites. She begins by describing her attempt to educate white jurors who are unfamiliar with poor blacks' lifestyles.

The main problem I had with the jury as a whole was that they were not considering what background this kid came out of. They were looking at it from a white middle-class point of view. Let me give you an example. There was testimony where they said that the defendant stayed out until eleven o'clock at night. But we are looking at a different kid here. This kid came out of a broken home where there was no structure, no authority figures. . . . He just came as he went. Of course he's going to stay out until eleven o'clock at night!

He's going to stay up beyond that. And they were arguing, "Well, my kid comes in at such and such."

Nevertheless, sympathy for her white counterparts gives way to frustration.

And I was frustrated. I felt there had to be more blacks on the jury. Because I think that was a big frustration for me. Because they were looking at this thing from a white middle-class perspective, and you have to put yourself into that black lifestyle this kid came out of. That particular lifestyle where there was not a good home, no supervision, there were no authority figures for this kid. So why waste time on talking about, my God, what time this kid comes in the house! There were a lot of little instances like that. That's why I felt like an outsider at times, because I felt I should have been more force-ful at trying to get these people to understand. We had to look at it like the lifestyle he came out of, the background he came out of. But nobody wanted to listen. They all wanted to talk. I'm not strong willed. I'm not forceful enough. That's why I felt like an outsider. So, rather than get into it, I didn't say much. I mean, I deliberated, but I didn't say much about those types of things. So that was a biggie, and it didn't make me happy. And I felt there should have been more blacks on the jury to balance that out.

Shirley Sharpe employs two distinct racialized discourses. On one hand, she speaks as an educated black juror who is sympathetic to her culturally distant white counterparts. However, on the other, she is unable to educate them on the realities of social disorganiza-tion and the absence of social control, so she turns to a narrative of resisting white racism. In this story, the problem with the jury sys-tem is all too clear: whites are too socially estranged from blacks to make sense of their murderous actions. Thus, Shirley Sharpe felt like an outsider who lacked the will to persuade the whites.

Moreover, it is important to note that this shift in her story from racial educator to resister is arrayed against the specific backdrop of being the only African American juror in this tale. Indeed, this reality and her failure to persuade the white majority helps to explain her profound sense of racial disconnection, which manifests in her own personal estrangement and ultimately in her feelings that the system desperately needs reform. This narrative shift can be heard as elucidating both a local and global consciousness. Such a "double consciousness" (DuBois 1981) as an African American capital juror and as a member of the black community helps to explain why black jurors may come to resent the white majority jurors whom the blacks see as utterly estranged from black life outside the legal system.

Bart Charles: "I Wanted to Go for Mercy in the Sentencing Phase of It, on Account of His Mother"

In other instances, resistance is mobilized as sympathy for defendants' family members. Hearing the tragic tales of the defendants' mothers, jurors and other allies may show mercy for defendants' lives.

> The majority wanted to give him the death sentence to begin with. But I was one of them that were not in the majority to begin with—I was in the minority. I wanted to go for mercy in the sentencing phase of it, on account of his mother. When they presented her and explained that all the other sons had been killed, that changed my mind from the death sentence to a life sentence.

However, Bart Charles, a white high-school-educated farmer, refused to take on the majority alone.

> Now, I wasn't going to be a lone holdout. In other words, I wouldn't have caused an opinion that another trial would come about it. But there was a Negro or a black, or whatever you want to call it, that was on the jury, and he did hold out.

> He said, "No way. I cannot consider a death sentence." So I went along with him on it, mainly because of the boy's mother. And in the end, all the rest of them came around to it, and that's what we gave him.

As an obviously less-educated juror, Bart Charles, in a bizarre and ironic turn, evokes the tale of an inferior race in describing how he was able to ultimately spare defendant Joseph Raymond's life. Indeed, the "Negro" also opposed giving the death sentence, "so I went along with him." Finally, Bart Charles describes how the majority changed their votes from death to life.

> I guess they didn't want to spend the rest of the week there or cause a mistrial on the account of it. Also, the law would be satisfied with either one. One of them was adamant about giving him the death sentence. He said that if Joseph Raymond did get the life sentence, he might be paroled and be a threat to society. My thinking on that was he'd have to be considered to begin with, and the people that would be considering him for parole would be responsible or take the blame for it if he was ever paroled. In other words, if he was ever turned loose, then the blame would be on them, not me. I'll tell you another thing—if they give him the death penalty, there is always the possibility of him changing it in an appeal, and usually if you give them the death penalty they appeal it. That thing goes through the court ten or fifteen years, and there's always the chance that they can change it.

Confronted with the tale of a broken justice system, Bart Charles resists the insiders' challenges: "If he was ever turned loose, then the blame would be on them, not me." Finally, in a fascinating demonstration of the instability of insider identity, Bart Charles co-opts broken justice as means for justifying his own decision to impose a life sentence: "There is always the possibility of him changing it in an appeal." Bart Charles "knows" that "life is not life" and "death is not death"—in effect, he is a sympathetic resister who beats the insiders at their own game.

Wanda Nelson: "They Isolated Themselves from Us. . . . I Don't Think He Should Have to Die Because of Drugs"

The government pursues the death sentence in a case with multiple offenders and no physical evidence; resisters tell stories of confusion and frustration about both the case at hand and the broader justice system.

> We didn't have the full details to back up everything. Sometimes our own government is responsible for the whole mess. I mean, look at what President Bush and his son were doing down there! Bush was allowing drugs to be brought into this country! And he and his son in Florida [Jeb Bush] were allowing this to happen, and it was Michael Sanchez and others that were bringing them in. But after it was all over, our government had to get out of it somehow, they had to do something, so they turned on them. I don't think that you should have to die because of drugs. My goodness, that was your choice to take the things! But if they were going to get out and sell them to kids, I would say they should be locked up for life. You know, a lot of us are responsible for whether or not we take drugs. You can't blame somebody who's out selling them.

As a juror in a federal death penalty case, Wanda Nelson, a white high-school-educated homemaker, expresses multiple frustrations about the government's case. Michael Sanchez, a Latino who smuggled cocaine into the United States from Mexico, was one of four men involved in a dispute that resulted in the shooting deaths of three American drug dealers. Like Bart Charles, she appropriates the narratives of the insiders—the story of broken justice and individual responsibility—to resist the prosecution's case. Infusing her story with contemporary political anecdotes, she blames President George H. W. Bush and his widely known sons for conspiring to bring drugs into the United States. Next, she takes a libertarian, antiprohibitionist stance: "A lot of us are responsible for whether or not we take drugs. You can't blame somebody who's out selling them."

Next, Wanda Nelson turns her anger on a court system she perceives as failing to equip jurors to make reliable decisions.

> I didn't recognize that Sanchez had just been traveling with these drug smugglers. I mean, I found out after the trial that he got caught in the wrong place at the wrong time. I had no idea of that. I don't think they instruct you enough before you go into jury service. [Asks interviewer] Do you have influence over policy? [Interviewer laughs.] Well, you can tell them that I don't think that they instruct jurors enough.

Wanda Nelson tells her story *with* the interviewer. Expressing her frustration at not being better informed about the case, she asks, "Do you have influence over policy?" Not waiting for an answer, Wanda Nelson attempts to bring greater weight to her argument: "Well, you can tell them that I don't think that they instruct jurors enough." However, her resistance tale changes to one of alienation and despair when asked about how the jury made its sentencing decision.

> I remember it very well because we were isolated—the black girl and I were not even allowed to sit with them. The ten of them went off to themselves and got in their little circus. She and I sat over here, and I told her, "Well, there's one thing for sure, I'm not going to vote for the death penalty." So [after] about three days and three nights of isolating themselves from us, the black girl kind of broke down. And then I broke down, and I said, "Well, what the heck. I'm not going to sit up here and send myself to the hospital." And they got into a little huddle over there and did all the talking to each other, and we sat over there. Then the black girl got sick to her stomach about the whole thing and went into the bathroom and was vomiting. And I went in there to help her. I got a rag and was washing her face. And they came in and told us to get out of the bathroom. I said, "She is sick. She is vomiting, and she is sick of this whole mess. And I'm sick of it!" And I said, "If you don't watch yourself, we are both gonna walk out of

here." It would've been a mistrial, and that's what we planned on doing.

Elucidating the isolating separateness she and another resister experienced, Wanda Nelson takes us into the bathroom with her ally. Threatening to "walk out," she maintains resistance against the insiders she has come to resent.

> They were a bunch of dummies. They didn't discuss anything with us. They didn't discuss anything with us! I hid from them one time, and they like tore the place up looking for me, and the foreman was just mortified. But when we were voting on punishment, I said, "We can sit here until doomsday, and I'm not voting for the death penalty!" And the black girl says, "I'm not either." So, they went and sat over in their little corner and discussed it all without us.

Wayne Fenwick: "Would You Throw the Switch Yourself?"

Wayne Fenwick, a college-educated white middle-class businessman, was the sole life holdout. In a story of maintaining his ground against the eleven member pro-death majority, Fenwick, like Wanda Nelson, brings the interviewer into the jury room. He describes his resistance to the majority's "only a recommendation" narrative.

> Some wanted to kill him, and some didn't want to kill him. Some wanted an eye for an eye or whatever their motives were. . . . In my mind, I couldn't kill him. I told them, "Put the kid in the chair. Now would you go up there and throw the switch yourself?" They said, "Well, that's not my job." I said, "You are doing your job now. If you say, 'Go ahead,' that's the same as if you are doing it. Before you do this, make sure that you can sleep tonight or next week or the rest of your life with what you've done. And later on, you better not think, 'This kid did not have a chance, and what have I done?' That was my presentation to them.

Colleen Kirk: "I Was a Probation Officer"

Colleen Kirk, a white high-school-educated social worker, describes her struggle to communicate her feelings of empathy to other jury members. Listening to a fellow resister's story of being brought up in an abusive family, however, she spares the defendant's life.

> I think as we discussed it and as we looked at it, I struggled with not letting my emotions and my own personal history affect me. There was one young man who had had an alcoholic father who was abusive and abused his mother. The difference between him and David Gomez was he grew up to be a pretty big, strong kid and had older brothers that finally stood up to his father. They told him, "That's the last time you will hit her." He was also into a lot of different delinquent behavior, and someone had reached out to him who worked with street gangs. He really befriended him and became a male role model for him. . . . He was feeling that David hadn't been given the chance that he had been given and that if someone had been able to reach him and offer him some counsel, support, and role modeling, that the shooting wouldn't have had to happen. See, David's father taught him to steal. . . . I think that was probably what partly allowed me to say, "Yes, I think he should be given life in prison."

However, Colleen Kirk is a former probation officer, and sentencing Gomez to life in prison provides her with little comfort. Indeed, she even wonders "whether we would not be doing him a favor to give him the death penalty."

> For me as a former probation officer for six years, I had seen several youth authorities. I had been to the state prison. I knew about what happens to sort of pretty, young boys and how they are used and abused. I really feared that was what was going to happen to David. So I really wasn't sure whether

we would not be doing him a favor to give him the death penalty.

Nancy McAdams: "You Know, I Was Raised in a Good Environment, and I Know Right from Wrong"

Resisters step outside the bubble of their lives, looking within and finding mercy for the defendant. Nancy McAdams, a white high-school-educated secretary, spared Mark Jarvis, a black man who shot and killed two blacks.

> The rest of us did not want to give him death because of his environment and the way he had been raised. He was very, very immature for his age. He was just not very intelligent. What he did was horrible, and he should never be on the street again. I know Mark knew better, and he knew what he was doing was wrong. But he doesn't deserve the death penalty. You know, I was raised in a good environment, and I know right from wrong. Mark, on the other hand, had been raised like an animal. He was out for survival, and it's sad.

Cindy Sanford: "It's Really Different Than Mark's Upbringing. . . . If You're Christian or Not, or If You're Rich or Poor, That Really Makes No Difference"

A second juror from the Jarvis case, a white college-educated homemaker, employs her identity as a "caring and loving mother" to express sympathy for the defendant.

> I have a boy who is twenty-four, and he still loves and kisses me and his father. We have a very loving family, so it's really different than Mark's upbringing. I mean, Mark was out all hours of the night, but if my son wasn't home after school, I would be scared something happened to him. I'd give him a few hours, and I would call the police.

Next, Cindy Sanford expresses frustration at what she described as the insiders' closed-mindedness.

> There was a few of them who said on the first day that he was guilty! And I thought this was wrong. I mean, they claimed to be very moral Christians, and I thought that should not be brought into it! If you're Christian or not, or if you're rich or poor, that really makes no difference. The jurors should be only there to make a decision about whether or not the defendant is guilty, and not anything else. That's probably the only gripe that I have. That they would make up their mind when there was no evidence on the table yet! They said, "Yup, he's guilty, he did it." I don't think they understood that we were talking about a life, and we were talking about two lives that were lost that one life had taken. Those who are responsible for picking the jurors should make sure that prospective jurors keep their religious beliefs out of this.

Giving Life

> Narratives can also be subversive. To the degree that stories make visible and explicit the connections between particular lives and social organization, they may be liberatory. Subversive stories are narratives that emplot the connection between the particular and the general by locating persons and events within the encompassing web of social organization.
>
> —Patricia Ewick and Susan S. Silbey,
> "Subversive Stories and Hegemonic Tales" (1995)

Voices of resistance are rare in the death-qualified community; resisters' stories typically have very little impact on insiders. However, what happens when a defendant is spared the death sentence? Previous research suggests that life is not typically imposed out of resistance. Indeed, the majority is more likely to cave into the minority out of fear of becoming a hung jury (Bowers and Steiner 1998; Sandys 1995). Furthermore, jurors will reluctantly agree to spare the defendant's life to secure a capital murder conviction on a questionable case (Bowers, Sandys, and Steiner 1998). Yet what happens in the rare instance of a successful resistance campaign? To shed light on this question, I turn to a case study.

The Defendant: Morris Green

As a child, Morris Green, a black man, had been savagely abused by his father. His father would often tie Morris up in front of his mother and sister and beat him with a broomstick. Morris was also forced to watch his father rape and beat his younger sister and mother.

At age thirteen, Morris Green, who had an IQ of less than eighty, was arrested for stealing a neighbor's bicycle. While prosecutors are allowed wide discretion to waive juvenile offenders to be tried in adult courts, under state law Green's low IQ made him ineligible for waiver. However, Green's incompetent defense lawyer never had his IQ tested, and Green was convicted and sentenced to seven years in an adult prison.[2]

Crime Story

Driving through an impoverished area known for illegal drug dealing and prostitution, Morris Green picked up a young prostitute, Sean Ray, a white male. After bringing Ray to a deserted location, Green handcuffed him to a fence, beat him unconscious, slit his throat, dismembered his body, and packed his remains in trash bags in the trunk of Green's car. After being on the run for several weeks, Morris Green ran out of money and gas and turned himself in to the police.

At trial, the defense did not contest Green's confession of guilt. However, the defense's penalty phase presentation was far more elaborate. Drawing on family members and a host of expert witnesses, the defense presented the jury with a graphic presentation of Green's many years of childhood physical abuse.

David Granger, a black college-educated attorney, describes his
clearest memory of the experience on the jury.

> Well, as gruesome as the murder was, the thing that sticks out
> the most in my mind was how the childhood of the defendant
> was just as bad. That is why the case is so compelling. The life
> that man had is incredible. You think of somebody who was
> a murderer and spent a good 70 percent of his life in prison. I
> mean, he was in adult prison at thirteen! I can't imagine any-
> body on that jury who was not affected by the crime, Morris
> Green's childhood, and by the incredible work that went on
> in the jury room. We really put in a lot of work. It was one of
> the most intense things that I've ever done.

Negotiating the triangulated horrors of the capital murder trial—
the crime, the defendant's childhood, and the jury's struggle to do
the right thing—David Granger steps into "the most intense thing"
he has ever done. Expressing revulsion at Green's gruesome murders and anger at a criminal justice system that imprisoned Green
at thirteen, Granger speaks as both punitive insider and as empathetic resister.

An alternative, hybridized identity is represented in the story of
Barrett Mannheim, a white, self-described "liberal" college-educated schoolteacher, who challenges what he perceives as a profoundly misguided legal system.

> He was in prison as a youth in an adult facility for stealing a
> bicycle! In the 1950s, if you had an IQ less than eighty, they
> would put you away in one of these schools. But they never
> examined Green's IQ! However, when a prison psychologist
> found out it was below eighty, he wrote a letter to a judge
> from prison, but the judge ignored it. I mean, the justice sys-
> tem using their own rules didn't help to guide this kid at all!

"Using their own rules" can be heard as powerful words of resistance. As a liberal schoolteacher, Mannheim turns the insider narrative of broken justice on its head. Recalling the impassioned voice of a civil-rights-era activist, he employs Green's story as the grounds for a more global attack on the failure of "their rules." Setting this narrative against additional stories of Green's abusive childhood, jurors such as David Granger vividly recount the horrible details.

I mean, the defense presented pictures when he was a kid. There was one particular one of him and his dog. He was dressed in a suit. He was six or seven years old, and the story was that his father killed his dog—no, it was a rabbit! He had a pet rabbit, and the father killed it and made the family eat it. And when the family wouldn't eat it, he gave it to the dog, and he wouldn't eat it, so his dad killed the dog.

But for Granger, the interviewer must hear other stories of Morris Green's abuse.

That was only just one example. I mean the abuse and the things the father did were unbelievable! Oh yes—his dad made Morris feel inferior because he was darker skinned than the others. His father made him feel he wasn't really a part of the family, that he was somebody else's kid. His dad was good with a knife. One time, Morris was getting into his teens—I guess it was right before he was sent off to prison or just when he got back from his first go around—and he was going to confront his father about the abuse of his mother. His father was sexually molesting his sister. And so his father took a knife to his mom's throat as Morris was coming down the stairs and he said, "Boy, if you give me any trouble, I'll slit her throat."

Articulating the extreme dysfunctionality that characterized most of Green's childhood, Granger's story is clearly more than just a simple recounting of factual details. As a black man, Granger's willingness to open himself to the finite details of Green's life is a marker for the juror's identity as empathetic resister. As will be seen, Granger's unique insight and skill as storyteller ultimately turn the tide against the pro-death majority. However, the liberal schoolteacher clearly was an important ally for David Granger. Employing his identity as a schoolteacher in a low-income community, Barrett Mannheim reflects on how the jury grappled with Green's family's economic and social marginality.

> The social status came out in terms of how they were economically deprived and nutritionally deprived. David and I were trying to describe to the others who had much better upbringings. We described the sets of urgencies that accompany those abusive behaviors. For some people, who were brought up in a more traditional or, for lack of a better word, normal, environment, it's just beyond their comprehension. They cannot even imagine such dysfunctionality. They can't get an appreciation when everything has been normal for them. They just do not appreciate the capacity to love, the capacity to trust. There are some people who could not see that because they just assume that that's an inherited genetic trait.

In a fascinating tale of intersecting identities, Barrett Mannheim as both jury member and schoolteacher struggles to educate the white jurors. He struggles to help the insiders see the "sets of urgencies" that are taken for granted by the privileged,[3] who do not "appreciate the capacity to love, the capacity to trust." Mannheim rejects the insider's genetically coded rhetoric of "inherited" immorality. Nevertheless, he remains persistent in his attempt to enlighten the majority but describes the insiders as very reluctant to relinquish their story of individual responsibility.

> There were a lot of individual-responsibility folks who were much harsher—"You do the crime, you do the time." It was more rigid and much more the individual responsibility, that

whole concept. "I don't care what your background is, you pull the trigger, you do the time. Whatever." I guess they were less educated. They had valid feelings, but they couldn't supply the same level of intellectual understanding to the whole process.

Observing that the insiders were less educated, he remains sensitive to their feelings, which he describes as "valid." Describing how the resisters eventually converted the insiders, Mannheim notes the vital role that David Granger as a black man played during jury deliberations.

I think most often it came from David. He would say, "You all may not realize that for a poor black person to do X, Y, or Z." In other words, this is how we as a culture might look only on this event and not the home situation, the dominant father and the matronly passive mother. A lot of people had anger towards the mother, saying, "How could she know that her daughter was being raped and never do anything? How could that happen?" So a lot of the whole flavor of our deliberations was trying to get an understanding. We were trying to make sense of these bizarre events, both the crimes and what led to his makeup. We were just trying to explain and understand how someone could do something like that and how could our society do certain things to cause someone to become like that.

In the end, in what is certainly a rare event—as the rest of this book demonstrates—the resisters prevail. David Granger's eloquent and impassioned story of racial and economic marginality persuades Gary Lombardo, the final holdout for death. As Lombardo, a white college-educated filmmaker, describes,

I was the final person to change my vote from life to death. It was a black juror, David. Oh boy, this is gonna sound really terrible when it comes out of my mouth! [*Laughs*] But it was his manner and charisma, his compassion and his articulation that moved me so much in regards to the black race in terms that Green was victimized. David was a black man who was almost in the same situation without the atrocities and the abuse and everything, but he grew up black, poor, and from the South. He led a very compassionate life. So, finally I guess after nothing more than a benefit of the doubt and compassion, I agreed it would be life without parole. David is a wonderful guy. He's a wonderful, wonderful soul, such a person.

While David Granger's eloquent voice of resistance persuaded jurors to show mercy on Morris Green, most resisters are not as successful. Indeed, like David Granger, they are overwhelmingly outnumbered. But unlike him, they do not possess the narrative capital to effectively persuade the pro-death majority. As I will show in chapter 7, when resisters are present on juries, their voices are typically discounted, rebuffed, or altogether drowned out in a cacophony of insider voices.

Doing Death

Up into this point, I have focused on jurors' stories, attitudes, and beliefs. While individual-level analyses provide a critical context for understanding citizens' experiences as capital-sentencing jurors, the decision to impose the death sentence ultimately rests in the hands of multiple jurors. In coming together to share their reactions to cases, to tell stories, and ultimately to agree on whether the defendant lives or dies, jurors decide who *he* (the defendant) is, who *we* (the jury) are, and how *we* should punish.

Chapter 6
Representing Death

Stories "develop" the relation between acts, actors, and situations
from some point at which the action and the situation might have
had multiple definitional possibilities to a point at which a dominant
central action clearly establishes a significance for the situation and
vice versa. This is what is often called the "point" of the story.

—W. Lance Bennett and Martha S. Feldman,
Reconstructing Reality in the Courtroom (1981)

In chapter 4, I explored the stories of individual insiders. In the
next two chapters, I turn to the stories of multiple respondents from
the same case. Drawing on trial transcripts, state court opinions,
and the jurors themselves, I begin my analysis of multiple jurors'
stories by presenting narratives of both the defendant's crime and
the trial.[1] This material provides critical context for analyzing the
jurors' stories of the defendant and their punishment decisions.

In comparison to the previous chapters, I am thus able to present
a far more nuanced window into the story worlds of death penalty
juries. How do citizens with different identities come to see the
defendant? How are insider identities maintained? In the next
chapter, I turn to cases where multiple insiders tell stories of handling resisters.

Ivan Strayhorn

The Defendant

Ivan Strayhorn, a black man, had been in and out of correctional
facilities and substance abuse clinics for most of his life. Abused by

an alcoholic father, he spent most of his life as a ward of the state, and for most of his adult life Strayhorn was addicted to crack cocaine.

Crime Story

After being paroled for possession of an illegal substance, Ivan Strayhorn moved into the house of his stepmother, Ruth Grier. During the first year that they lived together, things seemed to go smoothly—indeed, Strayhorn found a part-time job and was trying to stay off of drugs. About a year later, however, Grier began to notice that money was missing from her purse and confronted Strayhorn. Fearing that his stepmother would inform his parole officer, Strayhorn accused her of being a snitch.

During the confrontation, Strayhorn choked his stepmother and then bound her hands and feet with a telephone cord. He then dragged her downstairs into a basement bathroom and placed a portion of rope around her neck so that she could not fully extend her body. He then closed the door to the bathroom, went into an adjacent laundry room, and turned on the dryer to drown out Grier's screams. Returning to the basement to check on her several hours later, Strayhorn found that Grier had freed her hands from the rope, so he retied them, gagged her with a torn nightgown apparently found in the laundry room, and then covered her in blankets. Ivan Strayhorn left the house at approximately 6:30 P.M.

Returning to his stepmother's home the following day around 8:00 or 9:00 P.M., Ivan Strayhorn went into the basement and heard Ruth Grier screaming. He then restarted the dryer to drown out her screams. Strayhorn went back upstairs to collect some more of his stepmother's belongings to sell, left the home, and did not return until the following day.

Upon his return, Ivan Strayhorn went downstairs. Seeing that his stepmother was moving under the blankets, he turned the dryer on again and left the residence. He returned the following day to pick up his paycheck from the mailbox but did not enter the house. Later the same day, Strayhorn returned to the home with a friend, and they removed his stepmother's television, intending to sell it. Strayhorn left the home and did not return again.

Approximately two days later, Charles Grier, Ruth Grier's brother, received a phone call from his sister's coworkers, who were concerned about her prolonged absence from work. Charles Grier gained entry into his sister's home and, after discovering its condition, called police, who found Ruth Grier's bound and gagged body in the basement. The cause of death was later determined to be starvation.

Only hours later, while processing Strayhorn on an unrelated arrest, the police learned of the murder of Ruth Grier. After advising Strayhorn of his rights, they questioned him about the murder. Strayhorn subsequently admitted his guilt, a confession that was tape-recorded by the police with Strayhorn's permission.

Having murdered his stepmother in the course of a robbery, Ivan Strayhorn was charged with capital murder. Nearly eleven months after his arrest Ivan Strayhorn was being tried in a racially diverse northeastern city. Jury selection lasted approximately one week. While the death-qualification process was sometimes contentious—the defense was especially critical when the prosecutor struck prospective African American jurors—the final twelve were fairly representative of the county. More specifically, the twelve-person venire included eight whites and four blacks, seven men and five women.[2]

The trial was marred by several altercations between Strayhorn and the judge, including one incident when a brawl broke out between Strayhorn and four courtroom deputies after the defendant refused to take his seat. While this altercation resulted in a two-hour delay in the trial proceedings, the entire trial lasted only approximately two and half days. The jury took less than thirty minutes to convict

Strayhorn of capital murder and little more than forty-five minutes to sentence him to death.

Ruth Randolph, a high-school-educated black woman, begins by sharing her impressions of Ivan Strayhorn.

> He had a horrible childhood. His mother was a prostitute; his father was a drunk and beat them both. This poor child was a victim himself. And I do understand all that—you do have sympathy for a child that has grown up in that type of environment with no love other than what he had from his stepmother. So what made me so upset was why would you do that to this woman who was nothing but good to you? She never hurt you. It wasn't her that hurt you. It was your mother and your father.

In the voice of a grief-stricken "family member," Ruth Randolph "asks" the defendant, "Why would you do that?" Like David Granger (see chap. 5), Ruth Randolph allows herself into Strayhorn's world. Her story is one of tragedy. However, unlike Sheila Brooks's story of the "lower socioeconomic black group" (see chap. 4), Ruth Randolph expresses a deeply personal sympathy for the defendant. For Ruth Randolph, Ivan Strayhorn is not a black "loser from day one." Indeed, she struggles and ultimately fails to make sense of what Ivan Strayhorn is.

> I don't think he felt for what he did at all. He didn't give me that impression. I believe he thought he was going to get away with it because he was on drugs. He figured with the drugs, he could get off. But he was on crack. He was out of his mind. He didn't know what he was doing. But what was interesting about the case was for three straight days—the prosecution basically asked him, "Were you high twenty-four hours a day for three straight days?" And to me, he was not. He was coherent, because he knew enough to sell his stepmother's

television to get money. He knew enough to go through her pocketbook. At one point she was yelling down there, and he went down and stuffed blankets and trash bags against the washer to keep her quiet. He knew you could hear her upstairs, so that led me to believe that he was coherent enough to know what he was doing. He was trying to silence her.

Once again, Ruth Randolph makes no explicit mention of Ivan Strayhorn's blackness. To the contrary, her raceless variation on the tragedy of the disadvantaged tale is subsumed in a story of individual responsibility. An African American juror who is also "before" and "against" the law (see appendix B), Ruth Randolph rationalizes Strayhorn's abusive, tragic, "horrible" life that led him to kill "the only person that was good to" him. Even though she acknowledges that Strayhorn was "out of his mind" on crack, he still "knew enough" to silence his stepmother. Unable to resolve this tension, she acquiesces to the formal law and sentences Strayhorn to death. She mobilizes a death penalty law that both denies racial oppression and social marginality and blames what she calls the "poor child victim." Thus, as an insider, mitigating evidence is ultimately nonsensical to Ruth Randolph. Indeed, for her, sentencing Ivan Strayhorn to death was just a job.

I guess thinking over and over, rehashing that all I was doing was my job as a juror. I wasn't the one that was putting the guy to death, the state was.

Separating herself from the omnipresent state, Ruth Randolph mobilizes death as a bureaucratic task. The "just a job" story elucidates how she reconciles her confusion over Strayhorn's motives for killing his stepmother. At the same time, Ruth Randolph never resolves exactly what his motives are. "Just a job" as only a recommendation story allows her to wash her hands of any responsibility for imposing the death sentence. Even if Ruth Randolph never makes sense of Strayhorn's actions, the state, by default, does it for her.

As discussed in chapter 4, Robert Waingrow is a white high-school-educated construction worker. He does not share any of Ruth Randolph's sympathy or confusion. Waingrow draws stark dichotomies between himself and the defendant. He repeatedly reinforces his status as moral insider and Strayhorn's status as immoral outsider. Robert Waingrow's earlier story of black-on-black violence elucidated his subsequent vengeance tale of "not doing it gently." Here, he combines a tale of a threatening Other and racial inferiority to represent an altercation Strayhorn had with the courtroom deputies during the trial.

> During the trial, we determined he was a very violent person, because he jumped up and grabbed a deputy and tried to get the pistol out of his holster in the court, in front of everybody. It took six guys to subdue him. One of the detectives went over, and Strayhorn damn near got his gun and probably would have shot him. And the judge is yelling, "Get the jury out! Get the jury out!" And everybody is going, "Oh my God, oh my God!" People scattered like you wouldn't believe. This guy was big, you know. And these big deputies are jumping all over him, and he's just dragging them along, just like a gorilla. Like Rodney King—you know, the same situation.

Robert Waingrow's racial-inferiority tale speaks for itself. The black male body is but a gendered and racist caricature in his story. Drawing on the Rodney King spectacle,[3] Waingrow describes Strayhorn as an inhuman beast, a chained gorilla. If black-on-black violence was the story that broadly located Strayhorn's murder of his stepmother, then seeing Strayhorn in this courtroom altercation only confirms for Robert Waingrow what he already knew about black men "like" Rodney King. By contrast, Ruth Randolph does not see this incident in explicitly racial terms; rather, it confirms for her that Strayhorn must be a "bad kid."

> After the incident, they had him in leg irons, but they didn't want the jury to see them. When they would move him, they took us out, and when he sat down they brought us back in

again. But it didn't take much to figure that out. . . . He was a very bad kid.

"Just a Job" and "Rodney King"

Ruth Randolph and Robert Waingrow both voted to sentence Ivan Strayhorn to death but arrived at this decision along different narrative axes. While Ruth Waingrow remained undecided all the way to the punishment phase, Robert Waingrow was predisposed to giving the death sentence before the penalty phase even began.[4] The analysis of their stories fleshes out why and how their stories were so different.

Ruth Randolph struggles to make sense of Strayhorn's tragic life and the circumstances leading up to the murder of his stepmother. Unable to reconcile this tension, she employs an "only a recommendation" story to distance herself from the consequences of voting for the death sentence. In this way, the "capillary moment"[5] of Ruth Randolph's ultimate decision can be interpreted as one of simultaneous confusion about and relief from official responsibility.

In contrast, Robert Waingrow knows from the beginning who Ivan Strayhorn is and how to vote on punishment. Employing a tale of racial inferiority, Waingrow dehumanizes Strayhorn as a chained gorilla, like Rodney King. As Toni Morrison eloquently observed about the conflation of race and inhumanity in the O. J. Simpson spectacle, for Robert Waingrow,

> race is itself primitive. . . . What might be illogical for a white is easily possible for a black who has never been required to make, assumed to make, or described as making "sense." Therefore when race is at play the leap from one judgment (faithful dog) to its complete opposite (treacherous snake) is a trained reflex. From this reductive point of view blacks are seen to live outside "reason" in a world of phenomena in which motive or its absence is sheltered from debate. Or, as a William Faulkner character put it, "a nigger is not a person so much as a form of behavior." (Morrison and Lacour 1997, xi)

Gary White

The Defendant

Gary White, a black man, had been unemployed for more than a year and was nearly broke. However, White leased a car, apparently using stolen money.[6] Gary was using the car to run small errands and to make regular visits to his girlfriend and baby. While he had not made a car payment in several months, the reasons for the following murder are not clear.

Crime Story

One afternoon, Gary White decided to commit a robbery. He pulled his car into his mother's garage and put a rifle in the backseat. Traveling to Rock Creek Shopping Plaza, he parked in a rear parking lot beside Barbara Anders, a white woman. White got his rifle and approached Anders's vehicle, shot her in the head, took her pocketbook, and fled the scene.

Less then half an hour after the shooting, White was apprehended in the mall area. The police spotted a rifle and a checkbook in his car. The checkbook was later determined to belong to Anders.

White was charged with capital murder for the shooting and robbery of Anders. His trial took place in a small, racially diverse southern county. The jury was composed of nine whites and three blacks.

The guilt trial lasted less than one day as the defense attorney admitted White's guilt in his opening statement to the jury: "We are not here to say that Gary didn't commit this crime. We are here to ask you to spare his life, to have mercy on his soul."

A particularly vivid moment at the punishment trial involved the emotional pleas of White's grandmother, mother, and girlfriend. His mother, Delores White, tearfully asked the jurors to spare her son. In spite of what he'd done, she begged the jurors to find it in their hearts not to take her baby.

The Jurors: Gail Scuttles, Shirley Loman, and Wayne Nickerson

The spectacle of the threatening Other confirms the identities of both moral insiders and immoral outsiders. Sitting in judgment of Gary White, Gail Scuttles, a homemaker, reacted to White's mother's testimony and to the subsequent testimony of his girlfriend. Responding to a question about what witnesses backfired for the defense, Scuttles states,

> The girlfriend told about how good he was with her two children although they were not his children and how—what a good person he was. It was all well and good to hear that, but he perked up when the girlfriend got on the stand, and even when she walked off the stand he looked at her and gave her this grin and winked at her, and, I mean, he had no response for his mother, who was up there shedding all these tears for him. And yet he had this response for his girlfriend. To me it really showed the coldness of the man.

Gail Scuttles's story incorporates both threat and paternalism in representing White as an immoral outsider. As a bad kid, Gary White's threatening in-court behavior trumps any redeeming qualities ("how good he was with her two children"). "He had no response for his mother" is an observation steeped in paternalistic expectations. As an insider, Gail Scuttles need not know anything about White's relationship with his mother. That he "perks up" for the "illegitimate" single mother and girlfriend already confirms Scuttles's taken-for-granted assumption. Indeed, it proves that he is an immoral and threatening Other who is outside the moral order. Moreover, Gail Scuttles observes,

> I really believe the justice system does not have a very good rehabilitation record, and I couldn't visualize that he could

change in prison. I have to think about this boy's mother at that time, to watch her son behind bars for thirty years. I don't know whether that would have been any more merciful for her than to have the boy executed. At least then his life is over with. Time does a healing for people and their grief—not that she wouldn't have more grief at the time, but to burden her with this boy being behind prison walls and what he would go through. I think about my son in prison for all those years. Knowing what goes on behind prison bars, I mean, it would just tear me apart to think of him being in prison.

Combining the tale of broken justice with her own identity as caring mother, Gail Scuttles makes sense of her decision to sentence Gary White to death. In a bizarre tale of a "merciful death sentence," Scuttles weaves both global and personal themes that enable her to see the death sentence as no more punitive than thirty years in prison. The tale of broken justice allows her to quickly dispense with the thought of sparing White's life. Indeed, she believes, "the justice system does not have a very good rehabilitation record." Having clarified this for herself, Gail Scuttles can now focus on the "burden" placed on the defendant's mother. In other words, Gail Scuttles focuses on White's mother because as a mother herself, Scuttles can identify with the other woman's plight. Incorporating the story of the empathetic mother, Gail Scuttles "knows" that "my son in prison . . . would just tear me apart." Yet in a fascinating instance of perverse irony, her story, in effect, states without clarification that death is less punitive than life. Leaving the world of punisher behind, Gail Scuttles as caring mother sees sentencing Gary White to death as a "charitable gesture" on behalf of his mother.

In response to the question "During the punishment phase did any of the defense witnesses backfire?" another juror from the White case, Shirley Loman, a white secretary, stated,

His mother—really, his reaction to his mother's testimony. He was very unemotional through the whole trial, and when his mother got on the stand and pleaded for his life, and he didn't bat an eye, not a tear, no emotion at all. That pretty much put him in the electric chair. . . . The point was brought up that our friends and neighbors were expecting us to do the right thing, and I was very concerned that this guy could get out of prison. I mean, with his episodes of violence, we were really afraid of what might happen if he is ever allowed out into society again.

Through an acute awareness of the defendant's in-court behavior, Shirley Loman's story articulates a situation she perceives as having only one appropriate outcome (showing emotion in response to his mother's heartfelt testimony). Thus, irrespective of what the defendant may actually have been feeling, Loman's story reveals the subtleties of how the story of the threatening outsider alone serves to justify her decision to put the defendant "in the electric chair." Next, she evokes the broken-justice motif to conjure uncertainty in the reader ("if this guy were to ever get out") and to further legitimize her decision to impose the death sentence. Such a fear of early release, which is widespread among capital-sentencing jurors more broadly (Steiner, Bowers, and Sarat 1999; Bowers and Steiner 1999), helps her to make sense of her decision precisely because she "can't know" what might happen to this threatening defendant who "didn't bat an eye."

The defendant's testimony at the end of the punishment phase only confirms for Shirley Loman that Gary White is a threatening outsider.

He came up to this podium very nicely dressed with a long, legal pad and a Bible in his hand. He stood up there, and he read a statement that was obviously prepared by his lawyer. He said how sorry he was for this family and the other people that had survived, for the trauma that they had to go through. And I mean it was just—that was really the wrong thing for his attorney to do. Bad move. They could have told that young man, "You know, you are up there pleading for your life. Now go to it." I mean, "Really express yourself!" I guess it could have maybe been looked over by his attorney, but he certainly should have said it in his own words. He came across as so insincere. He was very insincere—no remorse whatsoever.

The story of a third juror from the White case, Wayne Nickerson, a white mechanical engineer with a graduate degree, reveals the pervasive way the jury's decision to impose the death sentence may be racially justified.

What was amazing was there were two blacks on the jury. And if they had guns they would go out and shoot him right now. They weren't about to take this at all. And I thought if anybody would have identified with the grandmother, I thought that they would. . . . And, again, I can imagine what was going through their heads, "That could be my son." I mean, they were relating to it. And I said, "Hmm, I don't know what they're going to say." When they got back in the jury room they were ready to hang him right then and there.

"They were relating to it" is an interesting variation on the story of the multiracial jury's decision to impose the death sentence. Like Fred Dawson (see chap. 4), Wayne Nickerson relies on a paternalistic dominance of care. He voices sympathy for "these poor women." However, unlike the "nice black lady" who needed to be coaxed into the majority, the black jurors in this case were committed to imposing death on "one of their own," thereby amazing Nickerson. Nevertheless, like Fred Dawson, Wayne Nickerson's story implicitly relies on a racialized expectation for doing death as a jury.

The "Caring Mother" and the "Bad Kid"

The tale of the threatening Other is a dominant narrative in the White case; jurors Scuttles and Loman focus on the defendant's lack of response to his mother's pleas on his behalf. As mothers themselves, the event unleashes in them an alternate punitive identity. White's response to his girlfriend but not to his mother activates Gail Scuttles as empathetic mother. Combining the world of juror and defendant with the world of mother and son, she employs a hybridized logic of punitive maternalism. As mother, she in effect nullifies her decision to spare the defendant's life ("I think about my son in prison for all those years").

At the same time, as punisher she evokes the story of broken justice ("I really believe the justice system does not have a very good rehabilitation record"). The illogic of death as maternal care and the ideology of broken justice as a choice without real options interlock to ultimately deny the defendant his complex human identity. Gail Scuttles accomplishes her identity as moral and caring mother and law-enforcing juror and thus accomplishes the defendant's immorality as bad son and criminal worthy of the death sentence.

Pedro Arenas

The Defendant

The same patterns are evident with Hispanic defendants. Pedro Arenas, a Hispanic man, had been in and out of psychiatric institutions for most of his life. Diagnosed as mentally retarded, Arenas read and wrote English at a first-grade level. He had never maintained steady employment and from an early age had been estranged from his family. His father left Arenas and his siblings when they were very young, and his mother, who spoke very little English, was unemployed and lived below the poverty line.

Crime Story

At approximately 11:45 P.M., Pedro Arenas went for a car ride with an acquaintance, an unemployed white man named William Darley. Arenas and Darley drove approximately ten miles before coming upon a white woman, Leslie Royce, walking alone on the sidewalk. Darley and Arenas apparently drove next to Royce, forced her into the car, and drove to a clearing behind an abandoned house. To keep her from resisting, Arenas shoved Royce beneath his feet in the front seat of the car, bent over, and held a knife to her throat.

Once behind the abandoned house, Arenas and Darley forced Royce out of the car and raped and sodomized her. Arenas then stabbed her more than twenty times and left her for dead. Three days later, Arenas took some of his acquaintances to view Royce's body. Two days later, one of Arenas's acquaintances called the local police and reported the crime.

The trial took place in a large southwestern county with a predominantly Hispanic population. The jury comprised nine whites and three Hispanics, six men and six women.

William Darley agreed to a plea bargain in which he would plead guilty to the rape charges and testify against Arenas. As in the White case, the defense did not contest Arenas's guilt. Focusing instead on mercy, the defense relied on his family's emotional pleas for mercy during the punishment phase.

The Jurors: Betty Alma, Lynette Worrell, and Damon Arthur

Insiders feel threatened by the outsiders, telling racialized stories of concern. Betty Alma, a white high-school-educated homemaker, described the courtroom setting during the punishment phase.

> I think the Hispanics were really, really together. They looked hard. None of them got up and testified on his behalf except his mother. She pled for us not to give the death sentence. When it happened, I mean, all the big husky people that were in the audience stared towards him and stared towards us.

It is interesting that Betty Alma finds it necessary to mention ethnicity. Calling attention to the "hard-looking" Hispanics seems almost to suggest a form of racial insecurity or anxiety on her part, revealing pervasive stereotypes of Latin American dangerousness at the same time that it creates a sense of urgency in her story. Indeed, being confronted by Others in the courtroom, as in everyday life, triggers white fears and uncertainty.[7] That is to say, ethnicity spoken as such calls attention to how grave her decision really was. Finally, calling attention to ethnic solidarity ("The Hispanics were really, really together") is useful in Betty Alma's account as a discursive device for distancing herself from *them*.

A second juror from the Arenas case, Lynette Worrell, a high-school-educated former youth counselor, comments on the defendant's threatening appearance in court. Responding to a question concerning the most important factor in determining the defendant's punishment, Worrell observes,

> The bottom line was we all felt he wasn't remorseful. He would do it again. He was a scary person that we didn't want to be around. We had an obligation to society to be sure he wouldn't be out on the streets again. And we didn't feel that life in prison was long enough. There was a strong possibility with good conduct he might be out rather quickly. If he had acted more remorseful in any way, that certainly would have been something we would have talked more about. . . .
>
> He was probably his own worst enemy. If only he had looked during the trial like he did during jury selection. At that time, he looked like a nice kid. I mean, during the trial he certainly convinced the whole jury that he was someone we would not want to meet alone in a dark alley.

Lynette Worrell describes the jury as imposing punishment based on the way the defendant "looked during the trial." Moreover, the threatening-outsider motif in her story receives greater resonance when she contrasts the defendant's appearance during jury selection with his appearance at trial. Fixating on the "scary" defendant that "we would not want to meet in a dark alley," the Arenas jury, as described by Lynette Worrell, in effect, imposes death as a consequence of courtroom demeanor. Combining the threatening-outsider motif with her belief that a life sentence would not be "long enough," Lynette Worrell's story might have been about any unremorseful defendant, irrespective of the circumstances surrounding the case.

In response to the question, "Was there any information you did not have about his crime that you feel would have helped in making your decision about punishment?" Lynette Worrell said,

> If he had shown some care for the victim—Arenas just did not care. I don't know if he was capable of caring. I work with mentally retarded people. Maybe he was retarded, and maybe he didn't have a very high IQ. It doesn't have anything to do with what he did.

Despite the defense's attempt to demonstrate to the jury Arenas's mental retardation, Lynette Worrell "knows" it doesn't have anything to do with what he did. Like Melvin Seagal (see chap. 4), Lynette Worrell as professional "diagnoses" Arenas as "incapable of caring." For Worrell, mental retardation is a thinly veiled excuse—a transparent attempt to hide this "scary person" *we* didn't want to be around.

A third juror from the Arenas case, Damon Arthur, a white college-educated airline pilot, tells an alternative story of the threatening outsider. Whereas Lynette Worrell does not mention specific instances of the defendant's threatening behavior, Arthur describes a situation in which Arenas charged the stand while his accomplice, William Darley, offered incriminating testimony during the trial. The influence of this episode on Damon Arthur's perception of Pedro Arenas as a threatening outsider becomes especially apparent when describing Arenas's emotional reaction to his mother's testimony during the punishment phase.

> He did break down when he saw his mom. I mean, he tried to get to her. But how do you read this? Do you read it [as] because he felt bad for his mother, or did he realize what he had done, that he might be sentenced to death? I felt definitely, if he could threaten a guy that was on the stand in front of everybody. And I know they look like that. I mean the judge, I know she saw the way he threatened him, because she was looking at us and looking back at him. And you can read it in her eyes, "Did you see all that?"

Arthur's story speaks for itself. While obvious as a stereotype, "I know *they* look like that" suggests a form of discursive backpedaling on Arthur's part. Indeed, such a phrase is similar to the claim "I'm not racist—I have many friends who are black," heard in contemporary white racial discourse. Finally, and perhaps most interestingly, is how Arthur justifies his interpretation of the "dangerous Hispanic" by recalling the judge's reaction and, indeed, by speaking through the judge's voice: "Did you all see that?" The "that" may be interpreted as "the threatening Hispanic who should be executed." Furthermore, the recounting of this event washes away any thoughts of redemption Arthur may have had—how he read Pedro Arenas's emotional reactions to his mother's testimony.

Racial Threat and the Professional Insider

In a fascinating contrast to the White case, the Arenas jurors racialize and thus dismiss the defendant's remorse in response to his mother. For both Betty Alma and Damon Arthur, the intimidating presence of the Hispanic community set the stage for who Arenas is. Indeed, Arthur's suspicion about how *they* look is confirmed by the judge's response to Arenas's outburst. Trying to look past how "they look," Damon Arthur legitimizes his own racial biases because of what he "reads" in the judge's eyes.

Lynette Worrell arrives at her decision to sentence Arenas to death along an alternative narrative path. Focusing on what she perceives as Arenas's total lack of remorse, she employs her identity as professional insider to refute the defense expert's testimony about the defendant's mental retardation. Without stepping into the specific details of Pedro Arenas's life, Lynette Worrell simultaneously dismisses his mental retardation ("It doesn't have anything to do with what he did") and confirms him as a threatening outsider "incapable of caring."

In the Company of Insiders

This chapter has focused on cases involving multiple insiders. Demonstrating jurors' alternative narratives of the death sentence reveals how representations of insider identities are polyvocal. Employing a variety of different narratives, the insiders see things differently but ultimately arrive at the same decision: The defendant is an immoral outsider who should be executed. Focusing again how jurors' stories of death may be represented across alternative narrative axes, the next chapter explores how the insiders simultaneously manage resistance and decide to impose the death sentence.

Chapter 7
Handling Resisters

Reason, in the end, derives its persuasive strength from its high
standing in our overt culture. It has that standing because that culture embraces low contradictory propositions. One is that we have
in our culture all we need to know to cope with the world and other
people. The other proposition asserts that this is a facade, psychologically necessary, but in fact so distorted that if one follows its
directions, disaster must ensue. Behind the facade is the "real" reality, accessible, albeit imperfectly, one to reason. This real world, of
course, includes other people's irrationalities.

—F. G. Bailey,
The Tactical Uses of Passion (1983)

Steven Ralphs

The Defendant

Steven Ralphs, a white man, had been in and out of drug treatment
and juvenile detention facilities for most of his life. Estranged from
his mother and brother for more than fifteen years, Ralphs took
residence in a small and somewhat rundown motel, Motel 20–20,
with his girlfriend, Wendy Kirkwood, a prostitute. Both were
addicted to crystal methamphetamine, commonly known as crank
(Chomet 1990).

Crime Story

Ralphs and Kirkwood, both in the beginnings of crank with-
drawal and desperately craving the drug, decided to steal a

car and sell it to a used car dealer, thereby getting money to buy more drugs. They contacted the owner of a motor home advertised in a free magazine they found outside a convenience store, and the next day, Ralphs met the vehicle's owner, Gerry Trent, a white man, at his home. The two men entered the vehicle together, and when Trent turned around to retrieve the owner's manual from the glove compartment, Ralphs shot the man five times in the back of the head with a .38-caliber pistol.

With Trent's body still inside the vehicle, Ralphs drove it approximately twenty miles to a deserted rocky area, backed the vehicle to the top of a steep sloping canyon, made his way inside the passenger's cabin, and then rolled the body out the backdoor and down into the canyon. Ralphs then took the vehicle back to the Motel 20–20 and attempted to clean the vehicle with rags and his T-shirt. Finding it nearly impossible to clean all of the blood from inside the vehicle, Ralphs tore out the carpet in the passenger compartment, but frayed ends of carpet and bloodstains remained. Finally, Ralphs drove the vehicle to a local used car dealer, who, suspicious of what he described as Ralphs's "frazzled" state and disheveled appearance, refused to purchase the vehicle. However, a few hours later, Ralphs sold the vehicle to Simon Delphi, whom Ralphs had met outside the dealership.

One week later police spotted Delphi in the vehicle on a local interstate and brought him in for questioning. A police sketch artist subsequently produced a picture closely resembling Ralphs, and Ralphs was identified outside of Motel 20–20 and arrested for the robbery and murder of Trent.

The trial took place in a large urban western county. The jury included eight white women and four white men. The jury convicted Ralphs in approximately three days. However, the punishment phase was delayed nearly two months after an earthquake damaged the courthouse. When the trial resumed, the jury only needed two days to sentence Ralphs to death. An important moment for jurors involved a defense psychologist's testimony regarding Ralphs's addiction to crystal methamphetamine.

The Jurors: Madeline Kraft and Stephanie Dambrowski

Describing the impact of the psychiatrist's testimony on her punishment decision, Madeline Kraft, a white college-educated woman, observes,

> The psychiatrist talked about methamphetamines and that they can make you not aware of your doings and such. I thought it was a crock. I used them when I was in college. When they asked me during jury selection if I had ever used drugs, I said, "Yeah, I have." So when I was listening to this drug expert, I was thinking, "Have you ever done this stuff? Do you actually know what it does, or is this all just textbook knowledge?" He knew nothing, because I had done this stuff. I knew everything he was saying was just so farfetched. I wondered where he got all this stuff! I shared this with the other jurors, because there was another girl who was also a former addict and an alcoholic. She was hysterical during deliberations and told the jury, "I've done this stuff, used it, done it, and I wouldn't say, 'Let's go kill somebody today and get cash for drugs.'" I never was up for four or five or six days as he apparently was. Even so, when you do drugs you know its illegal, you know it's wrong. So I just believe you're responsible for your own actions.

As a former drug user, Madeline Kraft mobilizes a story of individual responsibility. Both Kraft and a fellow juror who is a recovering addict "know" the truth about addiction to methamphetamines, including Ralphs's addiction. In this way, their experience is his. Objectifying the defendant's experiences with drug addiction—indeed, burying the life that actually lived such an addiction—Madeline Kraft is certain that all addicts "know it is illegal." Indeed, "I believe you're responsible for your actions" ultimately reveals her tale as artifice for a more explicit story of individual responsibility. Echoing President George H. W. Bush's words less than a year earlier (see chap. 2), she rejects—fails to even consider—the social history that gives meaning to the psychiatrist's testimony as mitigating evidence. Writing about the awesome challenges capital jurors face in making sense of such mitigation, including drug addiction and childhood trauma, Craig Haney observes,

> It is difficult to imagine how any jury could begin to meaningfully analyze and fairly assess a capital defendant's moral culpability and blameworthiness absent a painstakingly researched, thoughtfully assembled, and carefully and comprehensively presented chronicle of his life. (Haney 1998, 376)

Turning to her story of the jury's punishment decision, Madeline Kraft attempts to persuade a resister.

> It got real nasty. There was this lady who just didn't think he should be held accountable for all that he did because of his drug problem. We told her, "If you drink and get into a car accident and kill somebody, you're still held accountable!" And drugs are still the same way: Doing drugs is illegal, and you know it going into it.

Next, she offers a chilling account of how the resister was finally worn down by the majority until she tearfully complied with the death sentence.

> It was just real tough for her, and she went with the death penalty I think more so on pressure. It got to the point where everybody started yelling at her and screaming at her and said, "Goddamn, you're gonna waste all this time and money and effort that we've all put in!" It was a big strain on all of us. There is something missing that she just couldn't put her finger on, and we kept telling her, "What the hell is it that you don't see?" But in the punishment phase she just couldn't see

that he should be given the death penalty for something that he really didn't have a lot of control over. She really thought he was sorry and that if he had to have done it over he wouldn't have done it that way. Well, I said, "I don't believe so—he would have done it the same darn way!" She cried. We all cried. There was not a dry eye in the jury room. It was very emotional. And then I remember that she walks back into the room and announces that she will give her decision one way or the other. She was gone for maybe twenty to twenty-five minutes, but it seemed like an eternity. And she was crying and then says, "Death."

Stephanie Dambrowski, a white high-school-educated administrative secretary, offers an alternative tale of how the insiders handled the resister. Describing the jury's punishment decision, she interrogates the resister, whom Dambrowski labels as the defendant's caring mother. Challenging the resister as a deceitful impostor, Dambrowski observes,

She had this unnatural attachment to him or something. I think that she mothered him in some way. Do you know what I'm saying? It was like she had some type of maternal need to protect him. But she kept saying, "He wasn't a bad person. Yes, he shot the guy five times and pleaded for his life, but he's really a nice guy." [Laughs] What she was saying had more to do with him than anything she believed concerning capital punishment. Either that was the case, or she outright lied when she said she could go for the death penalty when they asked her.

As the tension mounts against the holdout, Stephanie Dambrowski, in a final attempt to break the caring mother, pulls the resister into the world of the threatening outsider.

We had been talking about it over and over again, and finally I said, "Just think if he took your son, and he held him in a small dark place and pointed a gun at him while he begged for his life for ten minutes. And then he continued to shoot him with a .22-caliber pistol. Tell me how you feel about that!?! Just think about if for a minute."

Mobilizing the politics of the insiders, Stephanie Dambrowski's "tough on crime" story of breaking the resister echoes Justice Scalia's punishment-at-all-costs tale of private vengeance (see chap. 2). Ignoring the resister's pleas for mercy, Dambrowski interrogates the woman as pro-criminal. Refusing to consider Stephen Ralphs's marginality, Stephanie Dambrowski in effect defends the insider party line.

Multivocal Moralities

Insider morality is not all of a piece; it is made real at the intersections of jurors' multiple identities. When confronted with a resister, the polyvocal tactics of the insiders become even more apparent. Madeline Kraft and Stephanie Dambrowski mobilize two voices of the insiders. Kraft employs her identity as former drug user to lend authority to her tale of individual responsibility. Attempting to persuade the resister, she draws on the visceral and far more commonplace tale of the irresponsible drunk driver to give her argument even greater resonance. Committed to the orthodoxy of individual responsibility, Madeline Kraft is both former drug user and law enforcer. At the same time, her story of Stephen Ralphs is one of dishonest junkie and lawless outsider.

Alternatively, Stephanie Dambrowski as crime victim advocate challenges the resister as a deceitful caring mother who is pro-defendant and antivictim. Confronting her with the horrifying story of the hypothetical murder of her son, Stephanie Dambrowski steps into the shoes of the victimized mother turned victim's rights advocate. Drawing on a terrifying tale of random and predatory violence, she forecloses the possibility that the resister's feelings of sympathy are worthy of consideration. As a tough-on-crime hard-liner, she constructs the resister as a weak and ignorant adversary.

Donald Carson

The Defendant

For most of their childhood, Donald and Rupert Carson, two white males, had lived in abject poverty and been physically abused by their alcoholic father. Their mother, a prostitute and drug addict, had abandoned the brothers when they were very young. After their father died of a heart attack when they were thirteen and nine respectively, Donald and Rupert Carson were placed in an orphanage, where children were often subjected to corporal punishment. By the time they reached their early thirties, the Carsons had extensive experience in youth detention facilities and prison and were incarcerated in a state penitentiary for separate violent felonies.

Crime Story

Donald Carson, Rupert Carson, and a friend, Homer Edwards, a black man, broke out of prison in a stolen car. In the afternoon, their car was almost out of gas. Believing that they had spotted a gas pump behind a rural mobile home belonging to a middle-aged white couple, Dwight and Emma Davis, the escapees stopped to investigate. Although there was no pump, they noticed that no one was inside the trailer and decided to burglarize it. Donald and Rupert Carson entered the trailer while Homer Edwards waited in the car.

Unaware that their trailer was being burglarized, Dwight Davis and his father, John Davis, pulled in behind the trailer. Donald Carson forced them inside at gunpoint and emptied their pockets. Dwight Davis was taken into the trailer's south bedroom, while John Davis was taken to the north bedroom. Donald Carson shot and killed Dwight Davis, and then both he and Rupert Carson shot and killed John Davis.

Dwight Davis's brother, James Davis, soon drove up on a tractor, walked to the back door, and knocked. Rupert Carson answered the door and ordered James inside at gun-point. James Davis was forced to lie on the living room sofa, where he was shot and killed by Donald Carson.

After Donald Carson went outside to move the tractor, which was parked in front of the stolen car, Dwight Davis's wife, Emma, drove up. Donald Carson entered the trailer behind her and accosted her. At the same time, John Davis's uncle, Everett Davis, and another brother, Thomas Davis, drove up in a pickup truck. Leaving Homer Edwards (now inside) to watch Emma Davis, Donald and Rupert Carson went outside to confront the two men and forced them at gunpoint into the trailer. Once inside, Thomas was taken to the south bedroom and shot and killed by Donald Carson, while Everett was taken to the north bedroom and killed by Rupert Carson.

Homer Edwards and Donald Carson raped Emma Davis on a kitchen table and then drove to a heavily wooded area several miles away, where Emma Davis was raped again. Homer Edwards then shot and killed her. The escapees abandoned their car in the woods and took Emma Davis's car, which they later abandoned. They then stole another car and were arrested a few days later, in possession of guns later identified as the murder weapons and of property belonging to the victims.

Each defendant was tried separately. By agreeing to testify against Donald Carson, Homer Edwards and Rupert Carson were spared capital murder charges. While Donald Carson was convicted in approximately two days, the penalty phase lasted a full week.

A key issue of contention for jurors involved the importance of mitigating evidence concerning Donald Carson's abused childhood.

The Jurors: Margaret Wentworth and Candace Ballard

Margaret Wentworth, a college-educated high school teacher, describes the scene inside the jury room during the penalty phase.

She and the majority believe that Donald Carson deserves the death sentence and are trying to convince a holdout to go along.

> One lady went bonkers. She was hysterical and just wanted out of there. She was talking about how he was abused as a child and everything—that the child abuse caused him to do all this. But that's no excuse! I'm sorry—I felt very bad that he had no life, but that's no reason to do what he did and enjoy it, you know? She really thought she could get out of it: She was banging on the door, yelling! And another person shared that she had been abused her whole childhood, and she did not go out and commit crimes like these, that she had pulled herself up by her bootstraps and worked hard and made herself a productive member of society. But the holdout was crawling up the walls yelling and screaming, and they were trying to calm her down by saying, "Nobody's threatening you, and you have a right to your opinion."

The confounding of insider ideology and punishment is powerfully revealed in Margaret Wentworth's story of individual responsibility. Pulling oneself up by the bootstraps, a timeless American maxim, is a dominant theme in how jurors accomplish identity. Writing about a similar dynamic in neighborhood watch members' discussions of community crime problems, Theodore Sasson cogently observes,

> The bit of wisdom that says "everyone's the same"—that from a moral standpoint the poor are no different from the non poor—derives from *individualism* . . . And the notion that people freely "choose" crime derives, in part, from the notion that people are responsible for their own welfare (self-reliance), and in part from the veneration people attach to the act of choosing (individualism). (Sasson 1995, 150)

Holding the marginalized defendant responsible for his actions is taken for granted in Margaret Wentworth's story. Describing the self-reliant juror who "had been abused her whole childhood,"

Wentworth quickly dispenses with the defendant's social history. Despite Donald Carson's prolonged abuse and economic and social marginalization, Wentworth ideologically wipes away his life experiences as an empty excuse. In this way, the story of individual responsibility reinforces insider morality, constructs outsider immorality, and denies the frequency with which capital defendants such as Donald Carson are

> brutalized and neglected as children, pushed to the social and economic margins of our society, and often mistreated by the very institutions we had entrusted with the task of helping them. . . . Study after study has confirmed the cycles of desperation, hopelessness, and violence; cycles in which many capital defendants have become enmeshed. (Haney 1998, 376)

A second juror from the Carson case, Candace Ballard, a white high-school-educated secretary, picks up where Margaret Wentworth's story of handling the resister leaves off. In contrast to Wentworth, Ballard has tremendous empathy for the resister's struggle with the majority. Remaining undecided until the jury's final vote on punishment, Candace Ballard tells a story of her own and the resister's struggle to come to grips with imposing the death sentence. She begins by describing the resister's reaction to a fellow juror's statements regarding child abuse.

> She wanted to go talk to the judge, because she felt like she was being coerced by the statements that were being made by fellow members of the jury. She felt like it was inappropriate that one juror brought up that she was abused. She felt like it was persuading the other jurors to give the death sentence. I think she and I had the same kind of feelings. Her husband was a doctor, and I think she felt the jury was acting inappropriately. It was pretty bad.

Straddling the edge of insider and resister identity, Candace Ballard tells an empathetic story of a secret meeting with the juror. After switching her vote to death, Ballard mobilizes a hybrid empathy-responsibility story of divine intervention that combines the mercy and criminal-responsibility themes discussed in chapter 4.

[The resister] was really upset. She came down to my room [in the hotel where the jury was sequestered] one night. . . . We were trying to seek answers and to do the right thing. We got together and studied and read from the Bible to get some kind of help there. We went to the Scriptures, and we had a meeting of the minds there. I told her after we had another ballot that I had changed mine from life to death. She said, "I am so confused right now, I don't know what to do." I told her that it helped me a lot to pray about this every night and to just ask God for guidance. I said, "Ask God, because I know that it's bigger than that. God will forgive us if he knows what we did was out of good intentions."

Combining the voice of empathetic resistance with the insider narrative of "only a recommendation," Candace Ballard mobilizes the divine to relieve the resister of any feelings of personal responsibility. Indeed, in this instance, "God will forgive us" becomes the currency for doing death. Candace Ballard mobilizes the divine as a means simultaneously for saving face with the majority and for receiving moral redemption after caving in on the death sentence. In a fascinating and contradictory instance, she accomplishes both her religious identity as God-fearing person and her institutional identity as juror—her belief in God cleanses her of the responsibility of sentencing Donald Carson to death. Indeed, Candace Ballard never elaborates on her decision to impose death, only that she believes her relationship with God will be maintained (she made her decision to impose the death sentence with "good intentions").

Nevertheless, the holdout struggles to come to terms with a decision she does not accept. Describing the building pressure from the judge to reach a sentencing verdict, coupled with the jury's emotional exhaustion, Candace Ballard elaborates on the chain of events leading up to the holdout's eventual compliance with the imposition of the death sentence.

It was just too much. I said to her, "I know it's hot in here and that we're all tired. The judge needs to let us go and get some rest." The judge was hoping that we would bring back a verdict on the sentence. He would call back every once in a while, but it was getting late. It may have been around nine o'clock or so. But we were all so emotional. It didn't take her much longer after nine to change her mind.

Self-Reliance and Divine Intervention

In the Stephen Ralphs case, insider identities were found to be fragmented and thus mobilized on alternative narrative axes; the story of individual responsibility achieves the same punitive ends, but it is represented from two distinct perspectives. In contrast, jurors' stories about the Carson case reveal how insider and resister identities are by no means mutually exclusive. Who a juror is has implications for how the resister is dealt with and for what punishment is imposed. In this way, Margaret Wentworth and Candace Ballard serve on the same jury, tell stories of the same resister, but arrive at the decision to impose the death sentence along vastly different paths.

Margaret Wentworth, who decided to impose death at the end of the guilt trial, tells a story of individual responsibility. Relying on the experience of a self-reliant juror who was abused but apparently turned her life around, Wentworth rejects Carson's marginality as a flimsy excuse. Echoing the tough-on-crime rhetoric that is a fundamental pillar of insider ideology (see chap. 2), Margaret Wentworth must see Donald Carson's crimes as the free choice of an "evil" individual. Defending both punishment and privilege at all costs, she legitimizes the death sentence with a discourse that denies inequality and thus blames Donald Carson for his own oppression and hence criminality.

Candace Ballard, an actively practicing Baptist, has profound empathy for the resister. Drawing on the divine, she attempts to spiritually cleanse the holdout of the onerous burden of imposing the death sentence. In this way, Ballard's story is one of "good intentions"—God will forgive her and the resister for sentencing

Donald Carson to death. While we can only speculate about why the holdout finally votes for the death sentence, Candace Ballard takes comfort in the divine for both herself and the resister. Yet on closer inspection, her religious ideology maintains her identity as an insider. Without addressing the defendant's marginality, her story is about punishing to defend herself as both religious and as someone who tries hard. As long as Candace Ballard can save her soul and encourage the resister to do the same, she sees herself as emancipated from the responsibility of sentencing Donald Carson to death.

Jesus Elisé

The Defendant

Jesus Elisé, a Hispanic man, left home at an early age to join a street gang. On many occasions, he would spend time drinking alcohol and smoking crack cocaine with his gang brothers.[1]

Crime Story

One night Elisé was using crack cocaine with four fellow gang members in an abandoned building. Maria Gomez, a homeless prostitute, apparently engaged in a verbal confrontation with one of the members and ran from the building. Following Gomez into a nearby alley, Elisé and his four accomplices cornered her, threw her to the ground, and raped her. Screaming for help and threatening to call the police, Gomez attempted to flee but was detained by the gang members. Elisé retreated into the building, found a rusted metal pole, returned to the alley, and beat Gomez to death with it. In exchange for a lesser charge, the four accomplices agreed to testify against Elisé, who was charged with capital murder.

The critical point in the trial revolved around the jury's sentencing decision. While eleven jurors voted to give Elisé the death sentence, one resister, a "foreign" man who apparently had recently immigrated to the United States, held out for life.

Florence Delbert, a white high-school-educated retired salesperson, begins by describing her impressions of the defendant's upbringing.

> They kept saying he was very poor and that his father was not in the home, his mom had to work all the time, and that he hung around with a bad crowd. Everyone was responsible but him. And I don't agree that that's true. I mean, if we as a society are going to say it is okay for poor people to commit a crime because of their less-than-optimal upbringing, then we're going to have a society full of murderers. I mean, I grew up in a very poor home, and we didn't have any money at all. It doesn't have any bearing, I don't think, on the basic questions of citizenship and morality. Right and wrong doesn't change.

Like jurors from the previous two cases, Florence Delbert presents a world of clean moral dichotomies—of insiders and outsiders and good and evil. Combining the moral panic story of a "society full of murderers" with her experiences as a poor person, she blames Jesus Elisé for his marginality as poor, drug-addicted Latino gang member. Florence Delbert mobilizes the story of individual responsibility to reject an imposing collection of empirical evidence demonstrating the negative social psychological consequences of gang life on the individual's life course (Hagedorn 1998; Rodriguez 1994; Sanchez-Jankowski 1992; Sullivan 1989; Vigil 1988; Williams 1989). Writing about the effects of gang membership on the lives of capital defendants, Craig Haney eloquently observes,

> Gang membership represents another short-term adaptation taken in adolescence and young adulthood by some capital defendants to overcome the legacy of their early developmental problems and the pressures of the communities in which

they live. It often exacts a significantly negative, life-altering long-term price. [Individuals] turn to gangs as a way of coping with the "multiple marginality" of the rest of their existence. (1998, 374)

Although Elisé grew up in an impoverished, gang-ridden barrio, his social history is reduced to a story of the denial of individual responsibility. In this way, Florence Delbert exacts as punishment her own insider privilege—a middle-aged white middle-class woman who was not marginalized to the extent that the defendant was and who overcame poverty in a vastly different economic period,[2] she nonetheless receives the state's license to condemn to death the immoral outsider. Denying the devastating effects of contemporary deindustrialization and the attendant oppression of the barrio poor (Bourgois 1996), Florence Delbert as insider imposes death because "right and wrong doesn't change."

A second juror, Stan Harris, a graduate-school-educated software engineer, describes the first time the resister was discovered.

One of the jurors held out—this guy from [another country]. He was an engineer from [company]. He was a very intelligent man, but I don't think he appreciated a lot of the unsaid things about the American criminal justice system [*laughs*], such as life does not mean life. And frankly, if there had been a complaint at that time, there probably would have been a mistrial. I felt like the jury badgered him to the point to where he changed his vote. He thought that life meant life, your whole life. It's probably not one of the things that you discuss or are supposed to discuss legally. But this guy really thought that you could sentence someone to life and he would be never released into society. And that was a problem.

A third juror, Eileen Berg, a white college-educated homemaker, was far less concerned about how the resister was treated. Expressing resentment toward the foreign man, Berg blames his lack of comprehension of the state's broken justice system on "his heavy accent" and "different understanding of some words."

He's a stupid man. I mean, the guy worked at like [a computer job] or something! You know he was intelligent, he just didn't have enough of a grasp of—you know?—I don't even want to say the English language, because he spoke English fairly well. He had a real heavy accent, but just his understanding of some words, his definition of some words were different than what our understanding of those words were. And so he had a little bit of trouble with that, I think.

Echoing Berg's sentiments toward the resister, Delbert observes,

I think he was probably a naturalized citizen as opposed to someone born over here. He was saying the same thing everybody else was saying, but he was confusing some of the language. . . . So we spent a lot of time backtracking, asking him yes-and-no questions and stuff to try to clarify what it was in our mind, because he was saying one thing—but then when it came time for a vote—he was voting differently.

Next, she rationalizes the resister's decision to change his vote to death.

He went around the room and asked people what they thought, and by the time he got all the way around the room, he changed his mind. He sort of wanted to do it that way. After we were unanimous, we were talking in a more relaxed manner, and he said that back in wherever he came from that Elisé would've been hung like the day it happened by people in the neighborhood. So it was interesting that after all that discussion about the following of the law and everything, I guess he just wanted to be technically correct according to what his instructions were. He was a perfectionist. I thought that was kind of amazing.

By contrast, Stan Harris's story of convincing the holdout had less to do with technical correctness and more to do with pressuring the resister into compliance.

Like I said, we probably broke all the rules. We had to give him a quick lesson in Criminal Justice 101 because he actually thought that life meant life. He believed you didn't have to kill somebody in order to be assured that they would stay behind bars with no hope of parole. This guy is obviously a danger to society, and we didn't have any other options. It was either life in prison with—which would have been a minimum sentence of twenty or thirty years, or it was death, which means, you know, as soon as you exhaust your appeals—maybe ten years. So there was a lot of frustration and a lot of hostility towards this person. We were very aggravated. I think there was a basic frustration on the part of the jurors. We were like, "What the hell are you even doing here?"

Educating the Resister

The story of a broken justice system is mobilized as a currency for breaking the resister; the insiders educate the foreign man that life does not mean life. Constructed as both alien to American culture and thus alien to insider ideology, the resister is represented as cultural outsider. Marginalizing the foreign man as stupid and idiotic, the insiders blame his lack of knowledge on his outsider status: He doesn't understand the language. Indeed, on closer inspection, the story of broken justice (life doesn't mean life) is transmuted into a profoundly racialized narrative.

What the foreign man doesn't know has everything to do with who he is not and who we are. But the jurors interviewed are careful to employ words of sympathy at the same time that they label the resister an idiot from another country. This is especially apparent in Stan Harris's final story.

But I think that we all understood that he was very intelligent, reasonable, compassionate person—not that the rest of the jury weren't, but he was more willing to exercise on the other side, a little more caution than the rest of the people, who were ready to string [Elisé] up. I think he truly believed that life meant life. He really believed that! And if you believe that, you are an idiot, or you just moved into the country and you've only lived here six months, which was his case.

Representing the resister simultaneously both as compassionate, intelligent, and reasonable and as idiot/foreigner, Stan Harris conflates the resister's identity with his decision to impose punishment. That is to say, by both accepting and rejecting the resister's Otherness, the insiders strategically represent themselves as both compassionate and intolerant of the foreign man.[3] But in the end, the story of broken justice allows them to distance themselves from such face-saving tactics. Ultimately, the defendant must by default be condemned to die because life does not mean life.

Barry Lawrence

The Defendant

Barry Lawrence, a white male, was one of ten siblings. Lawrence's mother was a waitress and housekeeper, and his father was a part-time truck driver. Lawrence's father drank and verbally abused his children. Moreover, working more than sixty hours a week, Lawrence's mother had little time to nurture her children.

A devastating event in Lawrence's life involved the death of his twelve-year-old brother. According to a defense psychologist's report, Lawrence and his brother had stolen a bottle of brandy from his father's room and had run off to a tree house, where they drank most of the liquor. While climbing down the tree house ladder, Lawrence's brother collapsed on the ground and stopped breathing. Overhearing Lawrence's cries for help, some neighbors called the police, but Lawrence's brother had suffered an allergic reaction that sent his body into toxic shock. He was pronounced dead on arrival at the hospital.

Unable to cope with his brother's death, a traumatized Barry Lawrence was denied counseling by his alcoholic father. According to the psychologist's report, Lawrence's father never treated

Lawrence the same way again and held the boy responsible for his brother's death.

Barry Lawrence dropped out of school and joined a motorcycle gang at seventeen. Two years later, facing prison time for stealing a car, Lawrence was allowed to join the navy. However, Lawrence's time in the navy proved disastrous: he was dishonorably discharged for insubordination only months after enlisting.

Crime Story

One evening, Barry Lawrence entered a convenience store at approximately 7:30 P.M. Waiting in line behind a customer who was apparently returning a videocassette, Lawrence without warning drew a .38-caliber revolver from his coat and shot the clerk, who subsequently died of gunshot wounds to the head. Although Lawrence reached for the cash register, the in-store video recording showed that he bumped into the counter and left the scene without taking any money. At trial, the prosecution played the in-store video recording as evidence that Barry Lawrence both intentionally murdered and attempted to rob the victim.

The Jurors: Henry Berry, Albert Reynolds, and Sandy McClintock

Henry Berry, a white college-educated business executive, describes how the jury made its punishment decision. Combining his role as foreman of the jury with his professional identity, he describes leading deliberations as a "professional workshop."

I decided that we should write a paper and title it "Norms." I knew from experience that it was real important that we equally decide in making the decision on the life of another individual. You know, "My vote isn't any more important that yours. So let's establish norms." And this is how we operated. We were all going to participate: "I'm going to give you

some ideas, and you are going to give some ideas. And everything on that paper is right." So then we worked on develop-
ing trust. I wanted people to feel when they contributed something it was just as important as anyone else. One of our
norms was we wouldn't attack any individuals personally.
We also had a rule that if emotion got out of hand, we would
break for five minutes, and that really helped when it happened. It was a wonderful calming device. So we kept those
norms on the wall, and we would always refer to them. It was
good because it put everybody on equal footing, and it seems
like it would be a model. I know I have used it to conduct
meetings.

Framing the jury's decision to impose the death sentence as a professional workshop or meeting, Henry Berry mobilizes his identity
as business executive as a means for doing death. However, when
confronted by a resister, Georgette Madison, Berry's "calming
device" is discarded for a story of "only a recommendation."

We had this juror, Georgette, who was an emergency room
nurse at some big city hospital who worked with little babies,
and she dwelled a lot on Barry. And she was saying, "I am
sending this person to the death chamber." But we were trying to separate that from what we were doing by saying, "It
was the circumstances that took place that is sending him to
death. Not you." We worked on that a lot with her.

Albert Reynolds, a white high-school-educated mechanic and Vietnam veteran, employed his biography to represent the defendant as
an immoral outsider and had an especially tense relationship with
Madison. He vividly describes an altercation between them.

She didn't like me! I mean, I thought he should die. I told her
my reasons, and she was like, "Na, na, na!" Sticking her
tongue out at me! She wasn't convincing. She was a nurse,
and she said she sees death too much, and she felt this was a
chance to give life. It was getting hot in that jury room! A cou-

ple of ladies told me I was browbeating her, and I guess I was—I mean, I can get pretty vocal. I mean, she was a nurse, and she was telling us how she held a baby that died. I told her that if she could hold a baby that died that never took a life and died, how could she want this guy who has taken lives to live? They told me I wasn't being fair to her, but she was the one who brought it up first. She kept trying to go back to the brother incident, and the point was made that he had sisters who didn't turn out like him. There are rough spots in life, but you just got to get around them and over them. She just didn't want to face that.

Reiterating his ability to "get over life's rough spots," Albert Reynolds as military veteran/tough juror marginalizes the resister as nurse/weak juror. Employing the story of individual responsibility, Reynolds dominates the nurse's empathetic voice of resistance. Undermining her experiences as a nurse as "not convincing," Reynolds turns against her. "How could she want this guy who has taken lives to live?" can be interpreted as a presentation of "normal" masculinity[4]—indeed, he can be heard as saying, "She wants him to live because she is a weak nurse who puts compassion over vengeance!" As a "pretty vocal" male who mocks the nurse as "pathetic" and "unconvincing" ("Na, na, na! Sticking her tongue out at me!") Albert Reynolds's tactics reveal the utility of doing masculinity as intimidation for mobilizing the politics of the insiders.[5] Indeed, in a self-deprecating twist, Reynolds acknowledges his wife's surprise that he was even chosen to serve as a juror.

My wife couldn't even believe that I was selected. They started with all 144 people, and we had to fill out this questionnaire, and I am for law and order. I guess I am a conservative in that sense, and they asked me if I was for the death penalty, and I said, "Yes." They asked me if I found this man guilty, could I condemn him to die, and I said, "Yes, in a minute!" So when my number was called to sit in that jury box, and I was never challenged, I couldn't believe it!

Like Reynolds, Sandy McClintock, a white female college-educated sales manager, expressed hostility toward the weak nurse. Here, she accuses the resister of trying to bamboozle the insiders.

> This one juror, she was a nurse, and she felt completely sorry for him. She made up this whole story about him that we had never heard before. She had this whole thing, and she had problems herself, and it became a whole case on her. It became fascinating from that point of view. I mean, she conjured up this whole story. The more we pressed her, the more she was digging in her heels. I think she was psychotic. So we were dealing with an unstable person, and the frustration that we all had as jurors was that we knew she was unstable! We all felt that all this time had been spent, and all this money had been spent on this guy who is a big loser! To us, it was pretty much black and white, and we had a pretty civil discussion, but she started talking about her twin sister that she lost at an early age and that she could relate to him. She was going off on such a tangent! That was so frustrating!

Sandy McClintock belittles the nurse as "psychotic" and "unstable." For McClintock, giving death is a "black and white" story of individual responsibility: He pulled the trigger, therefore he should be executed. Moreover, if the resister's remarkably coincidental story of losing her twin sister triggers empathy for a defendant who had also lost a sibling, then the nurse must be "unstable" and "psychotic." In other words, to resist the politics of the insiders is analogous to treason or at the very least to be constituted as psychologically unstable.

> The work of the denunciation effects the recasting of the objective character of the perceived other: The other person becomes in the eyes of his condemners literally a different and *new* person. It is not that the new attributes are added to the old "nucleus." He is not changed, he is reconstituted. (Garfinkel 1956, 421)

Next, Sandy McClintock mobilizes her identity as sales manager in an attempt to reconstitute the resister's empathetic identity through personal intimidation.

So, I was trying, from what I remember in my management courses, to persuade her. We started going over all of it again from square one. We would make up things to get her to come around! [*Laughs*] We would talk about how awful it would be to have this whole thing thrown out and retried because it was eleven to one. We really harped on that. We said, "This is our civic responsibility, and we'll just go forth," except she was adamant about life without parole.

However, when doing death as deceitful manipulation fails, McClintock resorts to an angry reiteration of the story of individual responsibility.

We were doing all kinds of things to turn her around because we were eleven to one. I just said, "No!" If we had to go through all the evidence again, and we are to come up with a decision, we are not going to cost taxpayers money. I mean, this was a black-and-white video! So I was getting pretty angry, and I was being pretty forceful. I just didn't want it to be all for nothing. I was thinking, "Now here's a case that is black and white, and we don't even live in a black-and-white world!" I mean, here's a case where we could actually see it on video!

In the end, the majority employs props to make the story of individual responsibility real to the holdout. After being forced to look at the gruesome autopsy photos of the victim, the nurse relents. According to McClintock,

The last thing we did was to bring in a picture of the victim's body, even though we had this big discussion about whether you could talk about the victim, and we were told you could not. So I said, "I don't want to talk about the victim, but I want to take a picture of the victim dead, and put it in the middle of the table." So we never talked about the victim, but we put it in the middle of the table all that day. That became real to her, and that was the part I felt she was missing all along. So, then Henry [Berry] took a poll to see if this woman could handle being polled, and she did it: She said, "Death."

Hearing the Voice of Resistance: Georgette Madison's Story

Georgette Madison, a white college-educated intensive-care-nursery health care practitioner, describes the first time she reflected on her experiences during the trial.

> After the defense gave their presentation, I would just watch his face, and it was such an emotional reaction. I really tried to play it down. I kind of said, "Well, this is a serious thing," but I really tried to play it down. At the time, I thought, "This is sort of interesting," because out of all the tragic things I've seen as a nurse—I mean, I am the one who takes off the tape and pulls out the tube, you know, "Oh shit! The baby's gasping still!" I can't understand it! I've seen tragic things. I mean, it's really hard when a baby dies, but I am always able to keep my professional distance.

In contrast to Albert Reynolds and like David Granger's empathy for Melvin Green (see chap. 5), Georgette Madison mobilizes her professional identity as nurse to bring herself closer to the defendant's social history. As a nurse she is able to distance herself from the act of taking a life. Indeed, as sociological studies of neonatal intensive care nurses attest, parental resistance to terminating an infant's life is negotiated as a challenge to professional norms.

> Members of the nursery staff respond to these micropolitical challenges to professional dominance by neutralizing dissent: they invoke psychological explanations of parents' behavior

that discount parental perspectives while defending professionals' worldviews. When they succeed the staff is able to defend their jurisdictional boundaries against parental encroachment. (Anspach 1993, 163)

When Georgette Madison encroaches on the insiders' decision to impose the death sentence, the tables are turned on her as capital juror. She is now the resistant parent, and the majority are the defenders of insider ideology. Rejected by the insiders, Georgette Madison begins to lose a sense of reality.

> I think as a nurse I can look at a person and see that they are in pain. I thought that was pretty valid. But they made fun of it. They thought that was the most ridiculous thing they ever heard. One guy got out his driver's license and wanted to know what I saw in it. The asshole! But then I looked at the picture, and I thought, "Maybe he's right?" I looked at this picture, and I sort of doubted myself, "Maybe I am crazy?"

Confronting head-on the responsibility of taking a life reduces the compassionate nurse to a crazy person. The insiders' degradation ritual pushes Georgette Madison to the brink of a nervous breakdown.

> I was like the weak and deformed person that society needed to get rid of. I think they really felt that they had a responsibility to society to make sure our panel rendered the death verdict. Surely, because they felt so strongly and there was so many of them, and here I was! I had a different opinion, and I was kind of shy. I was feeling extremely small and childish because here is this guy ridiculing me! I kind of just sat there instead of saying, "Well, goddamn it!" But I was feeding into it. I was really depressed. But I mean part of me was like, "You know, who cares if it's life without parole or death?!" I was very influenced by my thoughts. I was like, "Is there something wrong with me?" They were all so sure! And my hands were shaking. I had a feeling that people judged me as

being very sensitive and, um, that they kind of had a problem juror. I thought my brain was opening. I was so over-whelmed.

During sentencing deliberations, she turns to her family for sup-port. But her mother's story of a broken justice system does little to ease her conscience.

My mother said if he gets on death row, then he will probably never get executed. She said, "You know they sit on death row for years, if that makes it any easier for you." But during that night I made the decision that I had no confidence in myself. I was really full of self-doubt about my ability to give the decision.

In the end, however, Georgette Madison reluctantly gives her assent.

That day I wore black. Something in me that day didn't feel good about it at all. I knew something was wrong. I started crying pretty hard for a long time. So I finally decided to get up and go to the bathroom. I was just so overwhelmed by everything. I just felt wasted. The horrible bathroom—the whole scene—it was terrible. It was phony, and they were tired of it. They just wanted to go home. So it was sort of like going through the motions.

In the end, her story turns from self-anguish to contempt for the insiders. Describing the jury's entrance into the courtroom to give its death-sentencing verdict, Georgette Madison releases her anger.

And this other juror pointed out how they were going to poll us, and we have to publicly render our verdict. And then when we were walking to give our verdict and this juror started to worry about me! She said, "Are you okay with this?" I was like, "Fuck you, Bitch! Now that you have me on your side, you're worried about me!?!"

Chapter 8
Conclusion:
Pawns of the State

The Court next states that its unwillingness to regard petitioner's evidence as sufficient is based in part on the fear that recognition of McCleskey's claim would open the door to widespread challenges to all aspects of criminal sentencing. Taken on its face, such a statement seems to suggest a fear of too much justice. Yet surely the majority would acknowledge that if striking evidence indicated that other minority groups, or women, or even persons with blond hair, were disproportionately sentenced to death, such a state of affairs would be repugnant to deeply rooted conceptions of fairness. The prospect that there may be more widespread abuse than McCleskey documents may be dismaying, but it does not justify complete abdication of our judicial role. The Constitution was framed fundamentally as a bulwark against governmental power, and preventing the arbitrary administration of punishment is a basic ideal of any society that purports to be governed by the rule of law.

—Justice William Brennan,
dissenting in *McCleskey v. Kemp* (1987)

Jurors' racialized discourses reveal that the late Justice Brennan's fears in *McCleskey* were all too real but were more pervasive than he could have envisioned. The stories of capital jurors enlisted from a society that continues to be characterized by profound inequalities and a politically divisive climate such as that in the United States reveal that the death penalty is beyond "arbitrary." The imposition of the death sentence is not separate from the systems of privilege that have characterized and continue to characterize the prevailing social and political order. To be part of *us*, one must deny to others, often by default or personal reluctance, the privileges that enable one not to be part of *them*. Paradoxically, to know that there is a *them* is to know who *we* are.

The Grammars of Oppression

> What is happening here today is not injustice, but *oppression,* an attempt to throttle or stamp out a new form of life. And it is this new form of life that has grown up here in our midst that puzzles us, that expresses itself, like a weed growing from under a stone, in terms we call crime. Unless we grasp this problem in the light of this new reality, we cannot do more than salve our feelings of guilt and rage with more murder when a man, living under such conditions, commits an act which we call a crime.
>
> —Richard Wright, *Native Son* (1940)

> The in-group feels itself frequently misunderstood by the out-group; such failure to understand its way of life, so the in-group feels, must be rooted in hostile prejudices or in bad faith, since the truths held by the in-group are "matters of course," self-evident and, therefore, understandable by any human being. This feeling may lead to a partial shift of the system of relevances prevailing within the in-group, namely, by originating solidarity of resistance against outside criticism. The out-group is then looked at with repugnance, disgust, aversion, antipathy, hatred, or fear.
>
> —Alfred Schutz,
> *On Phenomenology and Social Relations* (1970)

Punishing identities are given life by an underlying grammar of oppression. As the state's death-qualified, the insiders impose the irrevocable sentence of death on the outsider because he, in effect, offends *us* under law. Dismissing the complex life histories of capital defendants as a "tragic" excuse or as confirmation that the defendant is a "loser," jurors' simultaneously reaffirm their identities as moral insiders. Within the specific contexts of their decisions to impose the death sentence, their identities as insiders are "actively utilized (rather than transcended) as a location for the construction of meaning, a place where meaning [is] discovered" (Alcoff 1988, 405). In this way, how jurors do death is a "multi-positional" accomplishment.

The multipositional self, then, is not only shaped by multiple histories, but shapes each and all of them. Rather than using history as a demand for change, it utilizes the experiences created by its history to negotiate with the categorizations that it embodies. (M. Cole 1999, 175)

Yet underneath the complex multipositional self that circulates within such punishing identities is a normative orientation to a prevailing politics of the insiders given legitimacy under the directive of the state. In this way, citizens enlisted as capital jurors can be seen as pawns in the state's game of lethal vengeance in the name of contradiction, confusion, and irrationality. The state's official line both enables jurors to distance themselves from the personal responsibility of imposing the death sentence (as only a recommendation) and forces them into a perverse zero-sum game of life and death, a game that brings out a myriad of moral justifications for the death sentence, including racially laced frustration and anger.

I don't hate anyone. It's the same bullshit that never stops. There's too much of it. Our welfare system makes these people. Our dollars we give them. It's terrible and awful. (Fred Dawson)

In short, the state sanctions the death-qualified to flaunt their privilege as punishment. From this perspective, the death penalty can be seen as investing in America's culture of inequality, particularly its ever-enduring color line. Racial inequality is protected in the lethal game the state imposes on jurors. The state in effect orders its citizens to mobilize their lives as arbitrary moral templates for measuring and subsequently dismissing defendants' lives. As Albert Reynolds's story elucidates,

I wanted to show my parents I could do something better in my life. Lawrence was also in and out of trouble. I felt sorry for him. I just wondered why a person would keep letting his life go on like that. Why didn't he just do it? I mean, you go where you have to. I took charge. I didn't let anybody control my life.

The state in effect orders capital jurors to reconcile the irreconcilable. As privileged insiders, typically segregated from poor whites or marginalized individuals of color (Massey 1995),[1] jurors are forced to rely on the only identity capital they possess. By employing the abstract currency of personal experience and common sense, they, like Ruth Randolph, a black woman who sentenced a black man to death, will never be able to articulate why they imposed the death sentence. As these passages from her interview attest, Randolph simultaneously speaks as empathetic "family member," insider, and subsequently pawn of the state.

> He had a horrible childhood. His mother was a prostitute; his father was a drunk and beat them both. This poor child was a victim himself. . . . But he was on crack. He was out of his mind. . . . He was coherent, because he knew enough to sell his stepmother's television to get money. He was trying to silence her. . . . I wasn't the one that was putting the guy to death; the state was.

Or the state's insiders may "know" precisely why the defendant should be sentenced to death. And when confronted with a resister, they may respond with "repugnance, disgust, aversion, antipathy, hatred, or fear" (Schutz 1970, 86).

> So there was a lot of frustration and a lot of hostility towards this person. We were very aggravated. I think there was a basic frustration on the part of the jurors. We were like, "What the hell are you even doing here?" But I think that we all understood that he was very intelligent, reasonable, compassionate person—not that the rest of the jury weren't, but he was willing to exercise on the other side, a little more caution than the rest of the people, who were ready to string [the defendant] up. I think he truly believed that life meant life. He really believed that! And if you

believe that, you are an idiot, or you just moved into the country and you've only lived here six months, which was his case. (Stan Harris)

The divisive and mean-spirited state-sanctioned politics of the insiders has a controlling interest in many if not most American criminal justice institutions. As I have argued throughout this book, punishment that disproportionately focuses on poor whites and marginalized individuals of color invests in a pernicious ideology of inherently moral insiders and inherently immoral outsiders. In this way, punishments such as the death penalty, the crack–powder cocaine sentencing disparity (Steiner 2001), and other overly punitive criminal justice policies not only inhibit efforts at social equality; the use of the death penalty in the United States undermines multiculturalism.

Multicultural discourse is the process of focusing on mutually beneficial goals, which, in turn, encourage people to listen to the storytelling of multipositional selves, finding value rather than conflict in the contingent and fluid experiences of individuals. If one person's individual experience can bring a new perspective that might further the mutual project, what becomes apparent is the value of that person's perspective, not its threat. (M. Cole 1999, 177)

By denying privilege vis-à-vis an inherently oppositional moral dogma, the state's endgame is straightforward: They deserve to die because they are inherently inferior.

From this perspective, it becomes clear how America's contemporary war on criminals is literally a war on equality: Such policies only serve to further open the politically driven chasm between *us* and *them*. In this way, heightened resistance to the politics of the insiders with the goal of eliminating irreversible and life-crushing punishments—the death penalty, protracted incarceration ("three strikes and you're out"), and antipoor policies such as "welfare reform"—is a limited but clearly important political step in the defense of multiculturalism.[2]

Privileging One Life over Another

> The right to life is, in one sense, antecedent to all the other rights in the Constitution. Without life in the sense of existence, it would not be possible to exercise rights or to be the bearer of them. But the right to life was included in the Constitution not simply to enshrine the right to existence. It is not life as mere organic matter that the Constitution cherishes, but the right to human life: the right to live as a human being, to be part of a broader community, to share in the experience of humanity. This concept of human life is at the centre of our constitutional values. . . . For apartheid was a denial of a common humanity. Black people were refused respect and dignity and thereby the dignity of all South Africans was diminished. . . . It must be emphasized that the entrenchment of a bill of rights, enforceable by a judiciary, is designed, in part, to protect those who are the marginalized, the dispossessed and the outcasts of our society. They are the test of our commitment to a common humanity and cannot be excluded from it.
>
> —Justice Arthur Chaskalson, South African Constitutional Court president, describing the Court's reasoning for making the death penalty in South Africa unconstitutional (*State v. Makwanyane,* 1995)

The continued use of the death penalty in America not only fails to protect "the dispossessed and the outcasts of our society" but under existing law invests in the privileging of one life over another. A response to this argument and the material presented in this book might be: Exactly—without the death penalty, society privileges the offender's life over the victim's life. Yet such a response fails to appreciate victims' multiple and often marginalized identities—indeed, who the victim is also has implications for what punishment the jury will impose, as Bernadette Garvin's story of a victim dying of AIDS profoundly revealed.

> During deliberations we had a whole gamut of things come out about sex, homosexuals, how men feel about homosexuals, and how women feel about homosexuals. That was one of the major things that happened. We could have gone in there if the man had not been a homosexual and got it done.

It would have been a much easier decision. But the minute homosexuality came in, and the fact that the man had AIDS came in, all the men went to this side, and all the women went to other. It was a pretty typical situation. . . . The men just couldn't understand that a murder is a murder regardless of whether or not the victim is gay and has AIDS.

Moreover, the argument that a murder victim's life is undervalued if the murderer is not put to death fails to appreciate the more profound story that I have attempted to tell throughout: State-sanctioned capital punishment forces jurors into an endless and arbitrary game of privileging one life over another. In this way, life is always at risk of being devalued—by denying the complexities of a victim's or defendant's marginality and disadvantage, the death penalty legitimizes inequality in the name of a privileged worldview based on the life experiences of jurors who have not experienced comparable marginality or disadvantage.

The human rights narrative presented by the South African Constitutional Court in its landmark decision to abolish the death penalty presents a grammar of justice. (For a review, see Bentele 1998.) This grammar is not unlike that found in the Declaration of Independence.

We hold these truths to be self-evident, that all men are created equal, that they are endowed by their Creator with certain unalienable Rights, that among these are Life, Liberty and the pursuit of Happiness. That to secure these rights, Governments are instituted among Men, deriving their just powers from the consent of the governed—That whenever any Form of Government becomes destructive of these ends, it is the Right of the People to alter or to abolish it, and to institute new Government, laying its foundation on such principles and organizing its powers in such form, as to them shall seem most likely to effect their Safety and Happiness.

Thus, for former capital juror Barrett Mannheim, the death sentence for Morris Green is anything but just.

For some people who were brought up in a more traditional or, for lack of a better word, normal, environment, it's just beyond their comprehension. They cannot even imagine such dysfunctionality. They can't get an appreciation when everything has been normal for them. They just do not appreciate the capacity to love, the capacity to trust. There are some people who could not see that, because they just assume that that's an inherited genetic trait.

The fundamental recognition of dignity in the "incomprehensible dysfunctionality" that is the lives of most capital defendants is the inescapable challenge posed by a broader human rights narrative against the death penalty. Beyond the current pragmatic but ultimately futile rhetoric of "death penalty reform,"[3] a human rights narrative recognizes the unearned privileges of social status—the lack of appreciation for the offender's "capacity to love, the capacity to trust." By defending human dignity, a human rights narrative[4] mobilizes just identities with the potential to transcend the polarizing narratives of us and them that are an ineradicable feature of the state's death penalty in action.

Appendix A
A Politics of the Insiders

Throughout this analysis, I attempt to elucidate the politics of the insiders as revealed in jurors' stories. By focusing on how jurors construct defendants as immoral outsiders, I often attempt to historically situate jurors' discourse in the broader political discourses that I deemed relevant for elucidating the connections among identity, morality, and punishment. In chapter 3, I outline more specific themes jurors' employ in discussing their sentencing decisions, but it is also important to briefly sketch the broader political economy of what I have termed a politics of the insiders. In presenting this material, I do not pretend that it is in anyway exhaustive. Rather, I am keying on a few historically situated examples that I believe are most relevant for understanding the period of discourse that I studied in jurors' stories (1991–94).

The story of the moral insiders/immoral outsiders alludes to a deeper, taken-for-granted hegemonic—a tale that serves to legitimize America's excessively punitive war on economically and racially marginalized outsiders. But to make sense of this insider hegemonic, one must investigate how a history of state actions has socially, politically, and economically invested in insider privileges at the expense of the marginalized and underprivileged. In short, an imposing body of research systematically demonstrates how governmental actions over time have divided the United States into a nation of unequal socioeconomic groups.

> The sedimentation of inequality occurred because blacks had barriers thrown up against them in their quest for material self-sufficiency. Whites in general, but well-off whites in particular, were able to amass assets and use their secure eco-

nomic status to pass their wealth from generation to generation. What is often not acknowledged is that the accumulation of wealth for some whites is intimately tied to the poverty of wealth for most blacks. Just as blacks have had "cumulative disadvantages," whites have had "cumulative advantages." Practically, every circumstance of bias and discrimination against blacks has produced a circumstance and opportunity of positive gain for whites. (Oliver and Shapiro 1995, 170)

Not surprisingly, demonstrating the color of economic inequality also suggests how such cumulative disadvantages result in the making and remaking of outsider identities ("criminal" blacks). The infamous Moynihan report is perhaps the most enduring public exposition of the story of upper-middle-class white moral identities and poor black immoral identities. Writing thirty years ago about the "subculture of the American negro," Daniel Patrick Moynihan observed,

A community that allows large numbers of young men to grow up in broken families, dominated by women, never acquiring any stable relationships to male authority, never acquiring any set of rational expectations about the future—that community asks for and gets chaos. Crime, violence, unrest, disorder, are not only to be expected, but they are very near to inevitable. And they are richly deserved. (Moynihan 1973, 31)

Moynihan's message arguably can be seen as a breakthrough discourse on the centrality of race and poverty in the political battlegrounds of U.S. policy reform. However, his implicit message of cultural inferiority has largely been co-opted into the prevailing identity politics of crime and punishment in the United States. Although the Moynihan report may have been progressive for its time, its central motif of culturally inferior blacks has become a pernicious part of American crime discourse. Indeed, as one of the key themes of the broader politics of the insiders, the devastating effects of social and economic exclusion and alienation are ignored by political elites who tacitly tell a story of "richly deserved" disorder and the need for harsh punitive responses. As the principal architect of America's contemporary crime war, President George H. W. Bush, stated,

> We must raise our voices to correct an insidious tendency—the tendency to blame crime on society rather than the criminal. . . . I, like most Americans, believe that we can start building a safer society by first agreeing that society itself doesn't cause the crime—criminals cause crime. (Bush 1989, 1)

Such a story of the insiders has been an indispensable way for political elites to justify the "dangers" of the outsiders and to simultaneously remake (in Bush's word, "We") insider identities (the "moral," "law-abiding," white middle or upper classes).

English Only

Another centerpiece of insider politics has been a growing antagonism toward non-English-speaking Hispanics. Such xenophobia has had its most public voice in America's growing English-only movement. As Alberto G. Mata Jr. observes,

> The English Only movement seeks to mandate English as the only language to be used in official U.S. business, including government offices and voting ballots. The movement reflects the fear that foreign languages might become more widespread than English, even though only 10 percent of the population speaks a language other than English. Of this group, over 13.5 million are Spanish speakers and only 12.5 million speak the entire range of other foreign languages. (Mata 1998, 147)

Thus, the racialization of Hispanics as dangerous and violent and subverting the English-only orthodoxy of the insiders further constructs Hispanics as alien. This insight is evident in my analysis of Hispanic capital defendants.

Moreover, the image of the illegal alien has been conflated with the image of the criminal, in effect providing greater meaning to the metaphor of the border in popular images of Hispanic criminals. Thus, it is not surprising that this alien-criminal conflation of Hispanics was codified under law as early as 1882, when Congress stipulated that "all foreign convicts except those convicted of political offenses" shall be deported (Mirandé 1987, 34). In this way, the threat of deportation can be seen as reinforcing the prevailing racialization of Hispanics as threatening outsiders. As Alfredo Mirandé observes in his classic book, *Gringo Justice* (1987),

> It is my contention that the "border experience" should occupy a central role in any conceptualization of the Latino experience, for there is a sense in which Latinos, try as they may, cannot divorce themselves from their Mexican roots. Despite efforts to merge into the melting pot by establishing themselves as "Mexican Americans," "Americans of Mexican descent," or just plain "Americans," the United States has been reluctant to incorporate them. . . . To many Americans they somehow remained "Mexican" or "foreign." (222)

Resisting the Insiders

In theory, death qualification is designed to purify the capital-sentencing jury of citizens who will resist the death sentence—jurors more likely to be cynical about state power, to be sensitive to pervading dominant-subordinate relations, and to have experienced marginality themselves are overwhelmingly deemed unqualified to serve and are thus vastly underrepresented on death penalty juries (Fitzgerald and Ellsworth 1984; Haney, Hurtado, and Vega 1994). However, the world of jury selection may fail to eliminate all "unqualified" citizens. Despite having said that one is in theory "capable of imposing the death sentence," facing the decision to condemn another human being to death may activate feelings of resistance. Resisters may challenge insiders' polarizing tales of morality/immorality. Having empathy for marginalized defendants or victims, resisters resist what they perceive as insiders' insensitive and elitist views.[1] However, are empathy and a shared sense of marginality sufficient for effective resistance?

Susan M. Olson and Christina Batjer's 1999 study of feminist resistance to a chauvinistic judge facing reelection in Utah elucidates the challenges entailed by successful acts of resistance. Olson and Batjer's research demonstrates the power of judicial impartiality as a hegemonic narrative. While feminist activists offered an effective although ultimately unsuccessful challenge to a judicial candidate, waging a successful campaign of resistance requires not only sharing experiences of marginality but also "tangible institutional support in the form of corroborating information and organizational resources" (1999, 145).

The politics of the moral insiders/immoral outsiders is how capital jurors do death; insiders describe resisters as behaving incorrectly or at worst as unqualified frauds who have lied during jury selection. Unlike organized resistance movements, resisters on the capital jury also lack the time and resources to subvert the insiders' stories. Chapter 3 explores the most common narratives employed by insiders in their stories of making the death penalty decision.

Appendix B
A Closer Look at African American Capital Jurors

> The boundaries thought to separate law from everyday life are understood to be relatively porous. The law as game involves a bracketing of everyday life—different rules apply, different statuses and roles operate, different resources count—but it is a bracketing that can be abandoned if need be.
>
> —Patricia Ewick and Susan S. Silbey,
> *The Commonplace of Law* (1998)

In chapter 5, many African American jurors were found to hold a uniquely resistant consciousness about imposing the death sentence. Their personal experiences in many ways provided them with a unique perspective on African American defendants and the inequities of the criminal justice system more broadly. However, to characterize all death-qualified African American jurors as opposed to the death penalty would be a gross simplification of these data. Indeed, a closer look at such jurors' legal consciousness reveals something closer to what I have argued from the outset: insider-resister identity is very pervasive and is often difficult to detect precisely because it is not all of a piece.

Here, I shift my methodological focus to explore African American and white capital jurors' attitudes and beliefs about crime and the criminal justice system. I seek to unpack capital jurors' complex and often contradictory perspectives on crime, the criminal justice system, and the death penalty. A more nuanced perspective of capital jurors' views in the abstract provides important insight for the analysis of jurors' stories, especially in chapter 6, where I investigate multiple and sometimes multiracial jurors from particular cases.

The Legal Consciousness of African American and White Citizens

The literature on race and attitudes toward the legal system demonstrates black and white citizens' widely divergent perspectives. Blacks are more likely to believe that charging decisions, convictions, and death sentences are tainted with racial bias, while whites are more likely to see the criminal justice system as excessively lenient and rigged in favor of defendants' rights (Lock 1999). Blacks have less confidence in the courts than whites do (Maguire and Pastore 1996) and are far less approving of the police (Huang and Vaughn 1996). While such studies are an important starting point for understanding the connections between respondents' race and their legal attitudes, these works tell us very little about what underlies such attitudes—indeed, these studies tell us very little about respondents' legal consciousness.[1] Focusing on law and the legal system as not separate from "everyday consciousness and practice" (Lazarus-Black and Hirsch 1994), sociolegal scholars recently have begun to demonstrate that public perceptions of the legal system are more complex than more traditional studies of legal attitudes would attest.

Patricia Ewick and Susan Silbey's (1998) seminal study of citizens' stories of their experiences with the legal system demonstrates a far more complex picture of legal consciousness. For Ewick and Silbey, law is a social construct that is constantly produced and reproduced. While citizens' multiple discourses about legality may reveal contradictions and inconsistencies, these discourses may also provide opportunities for resisting law's hegemony.

The same contradictions and openings that underwrite the operation of hegemony also make possible counterhegemonic readings and constructions. The recognition of these contradictions (i.e., that law is both a transcendent realm of rule-bound authority and yet available to resourceful players) are at the heart of resistance. (Ewick and Silbey 1998, 223)

Resistance, then, consists of comparing the incomparable, reconciling the irreconcilable.

In resisting hegemonic death penalty law, capital jurors hold, for example, a legal consciousness that both supports "tough punishment on the books" and mistrusts or is cynical about the legal process and its enforcement. While Ewick and Silbey do not systematically investigate legal consciousness across respondents' social status characteristics, this research does suggest that racial minorities tend to express a greater cynicism—that is, they rely more heavily on "against the law" in the telling of their stories (1998, 238). Thus, we might expect, especially in light of the jurors' stories of resistance presented in the chapter 5, that black capital jurors' will be more apt than whites to question the legal process in death penalty trials.

Laura Beth Nielsen's (2000) study of respondents' experiences with and attitudes toward street harassment provides further support for the expectation of such a race-resistance relationship. Building on Ewick and Silbey's study in a different legal context, Nielsen systematically demonstrates that respondents' attitudes toward free speech are far more nuanced than previous studies might suggest. Indeed, rather than a generalized finding of majority support for free speech, Nielsen determines that respondents may be both in support of free speech and "against the law." More specifically, she finds that white women and people of color are far more likely to experience racist and sexist speech from strangers in public and thus resist legal interventions—not as a matter of First Amendment absolutism, the rationale employed by most white men in her sample, but as a matter of personal empowerment and cynicism about the legal system. In this way, Nielsen's research, like Ewick and Silbey's, reveals the pervasively hegemonic character of free speech: lower-status respondents are both before and against the law.

As I argue in chapter 2, we might expect this death-qualified sample to hold punitive attitudes, irrespective of race. In other words, because the system selects only those jurors who can impose the death sentence, we might expect, as prior research with mock jurors demonstrates (Dillehay and Sandys 1996), that this sample of individuals will hold especially conservative, law-and-order perspectives, regardless of social status.

Are Capital Jurors before or against the Law?

> In what we call "Before the Law," legality is envisioned and enacted as if it were a separate sphere from ordinary social life: discontinuous, distinctive, yet authoritative and predictable. . . . Finally, we observed a third way of participating in legality when people revealed their sense of being caught within the law, or being up against the law.
>
> —Patricia Ewick and Susan S. Silbey,
> *The Commonplace of Law* (1998)

Are former capital jurors more likely to be before or against the law? To investigate this question, respondents' were asked, "Do you agree or disagree with the following statements about crime and the criminal justice system?" They were then asked if they "strongly agreed," "agreed," or "disagreed" with eighteen statements. For economy of presentation, I show only a selection of these eighteen statements.

PUNITIVE/BEFORE THE LAW (BTL) PERSPECTIVES: Agree with tough pro-victim punishment policies, cynical about defendants' rights and defense attorneys, and agree with strict enforcement of the death penalty.

Six of the eighteen statements tapping into punitive/BTL perspectives garnered majority agreement. More specifically, 81.9 percent of capital jurors either strongly agree or agree that convicted murderers serving life sentences should work in prison to provide restitution to their victims' families. Underlying this specific policy statement, jurors voiced nearly as strong levels of agreement with two of the other broader statements concerning murderers' debts

TABLE B1. Respondents' Beliefs about the Criminal Justice System and Punishment for Convicted Murderers (in percentages)

I. The Criminal Justice System

Do you agree or disagree with the following statements about crime and the criminal justice system?

"Even the worst criminals should be considered for mercy."

Strongly Agree	8.7	(N = 101)
Agree	30.6	(N = 354)
Disagree	49.0	(N = 566)
Don't Know/No Answer	11.6	(N = 134)
Total	100.0	(N = 1,155)

"The insanity plea is a loophole that allows too many guilty people to go free."

Strongly Agree	40.3	(N = 466)
Agree	33.9	(N = 391)
Disagree	14.0	(N = 162)
Don't Know/No Answer	11.8	(N = 136)
Total	100.0	(N = 1,155)

"Prosecutors have to be watched carefully, since they will use any means they can to get convictions."

Strongly Agree	12.5	(N = 144)
Agree	26.2	(N = 303)
Disagree	47.1	(N = 544)
Don't Know/No Answer	14.2	(N = 164)
Total	100.0	(N = 1,155)

"Defense attorneys have to be watched carefully, since they will use any means to get their clients off."

Strongly agree	21.0	(N = 243)
Agree	36.3	(N = 419)
Disagree	30.6	(N = 353)
Don't Know/No Answer	12.1	(N = 140)
Total	100.0	(N = 1,155)

"If we really cared about crime victims, we would make sure that criminals were given harsh punishments."

Strongly Agree	37.0	(N = 427)
Agree	30.9	(N = 357)
Disagree	19.0	(N = 219)
Don't Know/No Answer	13.2	(N = 152)
Total	100.0	(N = 1,155)

TABLE B1—*Continued*

"If we really cared about crime victims, we would make offenders work to pay for the injuries and losses their victims have suffered."

Strongly Agree	55.8	(N = 645)
Agree	26.1	(N = 301)
Disagree	6.3	(N = 73)
Don't Know/No Answer	11.8	(N = 136)
Total	100.0	(N = 1,155)

II. Punishment for Convicted Murderers

"You wish we had a better way than the death penalty of stopping murderers."

Strongly Agree	57.1	(N = 659)
Agree	21.9	(N = 253)
Disagree	15.0	(N = 173)
Don't Know/No Answer	6.1	(N = 70)
Total	100.0	(N = 1,155)

"If the death penalty were enforced more often there would be fewer murders in this country."

Strongly Agree	36.7	(N = 424)
Agree	27.4	(N = 316)
Disagree	26.8	(N = 309)
Don't Know/No Answer	9.2	(N = 106)
Total	100.0	(N = 1,155)

"Murderers owe something more than life in prison to society and especially to their victims' families."

Strongly Agree	42.9	(N = 495)
Agree	33.3	(N = 385)
Disagree	13.7	(N = 158)
Don't Know/No Answer	10.1	(N = 117)
Total	100.0	(N = 1,155)

to their victim's families (76.2 percent either strongly agree or agree) and the desire for harsh punishments as retribution for crime victims (67.9 percent either strongly agree or agree).

Moreover, punitive/BTL perspectives are indicated by high levels of agreement with statements tapping into opposition of defendants' rights, including the belief that the insanity defense is a loophole (74.2 percent strongly agree or agree) and weariness of "mistrustful" defense attorneys (57.3 percent). Respondents also express high levels of agreement with statements regarding stricter enforcement of the death penalty. More specifically, 67.3 percent strongly agree or agree that the death penalty should be required, and 64.1 percent agree that the death penalty should be enforced more often.

*CYNICAL/AGAINST THE LAW (ATL) PERSPECTIVES:
Agree that prosecutors have to be watched carefully and that criminals deserve mercy and wish there was a better way than the death penalty.*

By contrast to punitive/BTL perspectives, only "You wish we had a better way than the death penalty for stopping murderers" garnered a majority of agreement among respondents (79.0 percent). However, less than a majority disagreed with "Even the worst criminals should be considered for mercy" (49.0 percent) and "Prosecutors have to be watched more carefully" (47.1 percent). It is interesting that even death-qualified jurors, who might be expected to hold the least cynical/ATL perspectives (see Haney, Hurtado, and Vega 1994)[2]—hold such beliefs, as evidenced by their agreement with these select ATL statements.

Who Is before or against the Law?

To investigate levels of agreement by respondents' race, income, and gender, I first conducted factor analyses[3] of the eighteen statements. These analyses yielded two groupings of variables matching the six punitive/BTL variables and three cynical/ATL statements discussed previously. Table B2 shows results for a combined punitive/BTL index and a combined cynical/ATL index by respondents' race, income, and gender.[4]

Table B2 yields the following findings:

Black and lower-income respondents are more likely to hold strong punitive/BTL perspectives than are white and middle- and upper-income respondents.

TABLE B2. Punitive/Before the Law and Cynical/Against the Law Beliefs by Respondent's Race, Income, and Gender (in percentages)

	Race			Income					Gender		
	White	Blacks	Total	<30K	30K–50K	50K–75K	75K+	Total	Men	Women	Total
I. Punitive/Before the Law Beliefs											
Strong	23.2	34.5	24.3	30.5	25.2	21.8	19.5	24.5	24.9	24.2	24.5
Mod.	24.7	25.7	24.8	30.8	21.3	24.4	21.5	24.5	23.8	25.4	24.6
Low	45.3	34.5	44.2	34.8	43.9	47.9	52.5	43.9	44.6	43.7	44.1
N/A	6.9	5.3	6.7	4.0	9.6	5.9	6.5	7.1	6.7	6.7	6.7
N	(1,001)	(113)	(1,114)	(328)	(314)	(238)	(261)	(1,155)	(554)	(595)	(1,149)
II. Cynical/Against the Law Beliefs											
Strong	14.8	39.8	17.3	20.4	17.5	14.3	16.9	17.3	19.0	16.0	17.4
Mod.	32.1	31.9	32.0	29.9	33.8	37.4	26.4	31.6	30.5	32.9	31.8
Low	46.0	21.2	43.4	41.8	40.1	42.4	51.0	43.4	43.1	43.9	43.5
N/A	7.2	7.1	7.2	7.9	8.6	5.9	5.7	7.7	7.4	7.2	7.3
N	(1,001)	(113)	(1,114)	(328)	(314)	(238)	(261)	(1,155)	(554)	(595)	(1,149)

Note: For economy of presentation, I do not present the "No Answers" for respondents' income or gender.

*$p < .05$; **$p < .01$; ***$p < .001$ (significances are based on results from Guttman's coefficient of predictability (λ)).

In contrast to studies of the general population (e.g., Lock 1999), black and low-income respondents hold substantially more punitive/BTL perspectives than do whites and middle- and upper-income respondents. There is an 11.3 percentage point difference between racial groups: more than a third of black respondents (34.5 percent) hold strong beliefs, compared to 23.2 percent of whites. The pattern of punitive/BTL beliefs is equally vivid when contrasting respondents by annual income. The percentages of respondents holding strong beliefs represent a difference of more than 10 percentage points across categories (30.5 percent for those making more than thirty thousand dollars per year; 25.2 percent for those making between thirty and fifty thousand dollars; 21.8 percent for those making between fifty and seventy-five thousand dollars; and 19.5 percent for those making more than seventy-five thousand dollars). Interestingly, while prior research has documented higher levels of punitiveness among male respondents (Borg 1998), these data reveal no such gender differences between former capital jurors.

Black and, to a far lesser extent, lower-income respondents are more likely to hold strong cynical/ATL perspectives than are white and middle- and upper-income respondents.

There are substantial and significant[5] differences between black and white respondents' cynical/ATL perspectives. More specifically, approximately two of five (39.8 percent) blacks hold strong beliefs, compared to only 14.8 percent of whites. Moreover, this finding is amplified when comparing white and black jurors' low cynicism/ATL beliefs. More than twice as many whites as blacks (46.0 percent versus 21.2 percent) fall into this low category, demonstrating the racial polarization of cynical/ATL attitudes among former capital jurors. While consistent with expectations from prior research demonstrating greater black cynicism regarding the criminal justice system and its actors (Lock 1999), these findings are surprising given the higher level of punitive/BTL beliefs discovered in the first half of the table and the findings of unified strong feelings toward death as acceptable punishment. Indeed, given these findings, one might have assumed that being against the law would be rare among the death-qualified, irrespective of social group membership.

Moreover, one might have thought death-qualified black capital jurors would harbor beliefs more consistent with their white counterparts. Yet the data reported here tell a different story. Consistent with Ewick and Silbey's multiple-legalities hypothesis, these data demonstrate a contradictory consciousness among a substantial number of former black capital jurors, a legal consciousness that is in effect both before and against the law.

African American Jurors' Stories of Contradictory
Legal Consciousness

Many of the voices of resistance presented in chapter 5 were those of African American jurors. Yet the data here reveal that the legal consciousness of black jurors in the sample as a whole is far more complex than simply being pro-life. To elucidate such complexities, I combined both the punitive/BTL and the cynical/ATL indexes into a single index of jurors' contradictory consciousness and cross-tabulated it by jurors' race.[6] The results appear in table B3. More than twice as many black jurors as white jurors in the sample expressed a strong contradictory consciousness (42.7 percent versus 17.0 percent). Focusing on these forty-four black jurors with a contradictory legal consciousness, I closely read each of their interviews for discussions of both punitive/BTL and cynical/ATL perspectives.

Excavating such stories of law from the vast details of these

TABLE B3. Levels of Contradictory Consciousness by Respondents' Race (in percentages)

Levels of Punitive/Pro-Defendant and Cynical Pro-Victim Combined		
	Strong	Moderate	Low
White	17.0 (151)	30.4 (270)	52.6 (467)
Black	42.7 (44)	32.0 (33)	25.2 (26)

Note: Number of jurors is in parentheses.

forty-four respondents' interviews proved challenging. However, after several readings, I began to discover that they sometimes began to speak in the first person (e.g., "I have something to say about that"), signaling to me they were telling a story about the criminal justice system or other relevant legal experiences or beliefs. These stories were often rich in detail and communicated a number of ideas about the legitimacy of the law (63.6 percent) or respondents' negative experiences (36.3 percent) with the criminal justice system through the prism of the defendant's crime. Moreover, these stories were often rife with conflicting and sometimes contradictory statements. For example, thirty of forty-four respondents (68.1 percent) elaborated on punitiveness as a function of the defendant's specific[7] responsibility for the crime at the same time that they expressed discontent with the prison or legal system more broadly. Indeed, in the vast majority of these stories, jurors' articulations of what I call the narratives of criminal responsibility and legal cynicism are never reconciled—indeed, these jurors do not attempt to reconcile the seeming contradictions but instead draw from each (e.g., "He's responsible for the crime, but the system doesn't work").

For other black jurors, punitiveness was articulated far less explicitly. Fifteen of forty-four respondents (34.0 percent) struggled to determine whether the defendant deserved mercy as part of what

TABLE B4.   Total References Jurors' Made Suggesting a Contradictory Consciousness

	References (%)	N
[LEGITIMACY]	63.6	(28)
[EXPERIENCES]	36.3	(16)
[RESPONSIBILITY]	68.1	(30)
[CYNICISM]	100.0	(44)
[MERCY]	34.0	(15)

Note: While respondents may have made numerous references to these issues, the percentages presented here represent only one reference to the responsibility, cynicism, or mercy issues.

I call a moral-redemption narrative. At the same time, the jurors spoke of their cynicism regarding a broken criminal justice system that they described as ill equipped to bring what one juror called a "heart change" in the defendant. While more respondents focused on criminal responsibility than mercy (68.0 percent versus 34.0 percent), consistent with the statistical analysis, all forty-four of the respondents voiced some legal cynicism. The following section illustrates these conflicting narratives in the interviews of five of these forty-four respondents (11.3 percent).

Between Criminal Responsibility and Legal Cynicism

Despite being cynical about the legal system, how do black jurors make their punishment decisions? How is punitiveness expressed in their accounts of the jury's sentencing decision? How does playing the game of capital sentencing reveal an attitude that is what Ewick and Silbey (1998, 108–29) call "with the law?" The answer to this question is complex. First, black jurors focus on the level of the defendant's responsibility for the crime. Depending on the facts of the case, they are either convinced that the defendant is responsible or they express lingering doubts about his guilt.[8] However, in both instances, when jurors begin to reflect on the appropriate punishment for the defendant, they voice cynicism about the system's ability to dispense meaningful or reliable justice.

To highlight the voices of resistance, chapter 5 presented the views of two African American jurors, Harold Brown and Ronald Fredrickson. Both of these jurors articulated narratives of resisting white racism. Presenting descriptions and details of a kind of racial elitism that is perpetrated by disproportionately white middle- and upper-class suburbanite jurors, these men describe the jury as being incapable of meaningfully judging African American defendants in capital cases. Indeed, these resisting-white-racism narratives were found to reveal frustrated, angry, and despairing voices reminiscent of those heard in the period leading up to the civil rights movement of the 1960s.

Yet the complexities of the crime of which he sat in judgment forced Brown to simultaneously reflect on whether failing to sentence the defendant to death would constitute a continuing threat to society.

> Like I said, after killing four people, I don't think killing four more people would be a problem to him. . . . Like he said, he laughs when he kills niggers. He enjoys it. Those were his words: "I enjoy it. I always laugh when I kill people." Somebody [on the jury] said that's sick. That's not sick—he knows what he's doing. It's funny to him. May not be funny to you and me, but it was funny to him. Would he do it again? Sure he would.

As threatening as Brown finds the defendant, when describing the punishment decision, the juror expresses cynicism about the reliability of the death penalty.

> To me, I believe in capital punishment. I believe in an eye for an eye. The only problem with that is nothing is foolproof, nothing is guaranteed. There might be a situation where you execute a person and you find out later that the person didn't do it. I am sure you read about that every day.

Here, Harold Brown's responses reveal both punitive and cynical orientations to death penalty law. On the one hand, he is before the law in that he describes himself as focusing on the defendant's dangerousness and "an eye for an eye." On the other hand, Brown is also cynical about the reliability of the death sentence ("Nothing is foolproof").

For other jurors, the defendant's criminal responsibility is less clear-cut. According to Ronald Fredrickson, defendant Arthur Chester

> was the type who saved a lot of people's lives from this other boy [the codefendant]. He was charged with first-degree murder because he was with that other guy, and they made it seem like it was planned when they killed the cop. [Chester]

shouldn't have the death penalty. Every man should pay his own dues. He didn't hold the other guy's hand on the trigger.

In addition to Fredrickson's voice of resistance against those white jurors who wanted "fry those black boys" (see chap. 5), his doubts about Chester's guilt imply deep cynicism about the legitimacy of the state's felony murder law ("Every man should pay his own dues"). Indeed, Fredrickson's story reveals a more conflicted legal consciousness when asked to describe his punishment decision.

> I don't think [Chester] will ever be a citizen. He will probably be a criminal for the rest of his life. I'm not saying he was a good guy—by no means. I'm saying I don't think he should die for something someone else did. . . . You have different types of criminals: criminals who will kill someone, those who will rob stores. . . . Now, he would really kill somebody, I really believe that. But he would have to be highly provoked to do that.

Ronald Fredrickson knows the difference between a criminal and a citizen. For him, the offender is a criminal but not a cold-blooded murderer. Combining this and his previous narrative reveals a highly nuanced, hybridized logic of criminal responsibility/legal cynicism. In this way, Ronald Fredrickson is both before and against the law. Indeed, when he is asked how important the defendant's "background of extreme poverty" was as a factor in making his sentencing decision, he shifts back to a far more explicitly ideological commitment to a belief in individual responsibility for crime.

> Because a person is in poverty, it doesn't give you the right to kill someone. We all have rough times. Whether you're black, white, purple, or green, you are going to have rough times. This doesn't give you the right to take someone's life because of the times. You should go out and make those times better for yourself or try to work within yourself to make them better. It doesn't give you the right to kill someone.

For other African American jurors, like Theodore Willis, a truck driver who served on the case of Thomas Frank, a white man convicted of murdering his parents and brother, the death penalty fails both to deter future crime and to force the defendant to take responsibility for his actions. In describing his courtroom experiences, Willis tells a vivid against-the-law story of how seeing the defendant before and during the trial made this clear.

> If the death penalty really was a deterrent to killing again, the death of Mr. Frank would be more punishment than letting Mr. Frank rot in jail. So, I said to myself, "Okay, what are you gonna do? You want to take him out of society because he killed some people, or do you want to see him punished?" I'll give him a chance to repent, be sorry for what he had done. I'll give him some time to think about it. To me, that's punishment.

Resisting the death penalty, Willis, a self-described religious person, mobilizes a personal preference for repentance as law. As a counterhegemonic, Willis's story privileges mercy over the official law's call for retribution ("I'll give him some time to think about it").

Between Legal Cynicism and Moral Redemption

Black jurors who are both before and against the law may also tell stories that articulate a sense of frustration about whether the defendant might be redeemed. Rather than a more explicit elaboration of being before the law, these respondents tell stories that often invoke deeply religious beliefs regarding the defendant's moral redemption—in effect, they tell stories of being before God. However, these jurors still express a deep cynicism about the prison system, and this cynicism is often expressed in stories of their spirituality or of negative experiences with crime in their communities that have soured their belief in a just system.

Ophelia Street, a seamstress, served on the case of Morris Sanford, a black man convicted of killing a black female in a drug-related shooting. Responding to a question about whether she believed the defendant would be a "continuing threat to society," Street explained,

> If they are on drugs, they have a tendency, if they don't work, they are stealing, robbing, sticking you up to get money, your money. See these here bars I have on my house, that's why I am barred up now, for breaking into my house. You gotta be a prisoner in your own house, and you got to pay for them being in jail. I got [the bars] all around. I had to do that all on the first floor. A few years back, we were broken into three times in twenty-four days. I thought I'd lose my mind. We had to get bars. You have to be in jail in your own house and pay for them to be in prison. He gets free light and electricity and all.

Ophelia Street's story is one of both cynicism and punitive feelings of anger toward criminals in particular and the criminal justice system in general. Street reinforces her identity as a law-abiding, moral citizen and the defendant's identity as part of a stereotypical *them* ("If they are on drugs, they have a tendency, if they don't work, they are stealing, robbing, sticking you up to get money, your money"). Employing her personal identity as law-abiding citizen in her story of being a prisoner in her own house, she powerfully conveys a deep, moral concern about the crime problem. At the same time, Ophelia Street is angered about having "to pay for them being in jail." Yet being doubly victimized by criminals and the criminal justice system is not enough to overshadow Ophelia Street's deeply religious convictions. Mobilizing her religious identity, she comes to know who the defendant is and thus what punishment he deserves. She describes her feelings about giving the defendant a life sentence.

> I am a churchgoing person, and you gotta have forgiveness in your heart. You have to go up to that judgment bar. You have to give account. But [the defendant] just didn't care. If he goes to jail, he can sleep, eat. He has no gas, no electricity to take

care of. At least he is still living. The worst he has to worry about is somebody beating him up.

In this way, Ophelia Street as churchgoer trumps her identity as juror. By resisting official law as a response to the crime problem, she mobilizes her belief in forgiveness against the death sentence. Indeed, as tough and concerned about crime as she presents herself in her first story, her religious identity enables her to reconcile the seemingly irreconcilable death penalty and decides to spare the defendant's life.

Another black respondent, Dexter Megget, a construction worker who served on the case of Toby Leeson, a black man convicted of shooting a white police officer, explicitly links belief in redemption with a cynicism about the criminal justice system. More specifically, Megget's story focuses on his deeply Christian identity, his experiences with religious transformation, and his cynicism about the prison system's ability to facilitate a meaningful change in the defendant. Describing the importance of rehabilitation in the decision to spare the defendant's life, Megget explains,

> I will say that he can change but not the way the system helps. He has to have a heart change. He has to be changed inwardly in order for him to act right. The only way he can change inwardly is to have a personal relationship with Jesus—to receive Jesus Christ as Lord and Savior. He has to have an inward change. The only thing that is going to help that man is for him to change on the inside. We change from the inside, and it flows out the outside. So him being rehabilitated in the prison is not important. In my own life, I had an inward change, and it flowed to the outside. But the way the system is trying to help people, you know, I don't think it's doing a lot of good.

Like Ophelia Street, Dexter Megget reveals how multiple identities are at the core of holding a contradictory legal consciousness. He begins by expressing his beliefs about what it will take for the defendant to change. Revealing a religiously informed perspective, Megget as proselytizer starts his story by describing the need for the defendant "to receive Jesus as Lord and Savior." Megget then buttresses this point by describing his religious identity. Moving seamlessly from broad religious beliefs to his experiences as a person who was an immoral outsider but had an "inward change," Megget's story builds a sense of tension in the reader—the juror's biographical experiences help to reinforce his story's cynical conclusion: "The way the system is trying to help people, you know, I don't think it's doing a lot of good."[9]

Despite significant differences between black and white respondents' attitudes with respect to legal cynicism/against the law, I have found no significant differences in respondents' punitive/before-the-law perspectives. With very little variation, all respondents held strongly punitive views. Members of a historically underprivileged group are more likely to agree that prosecutors have to be watched carefully and that criminals deserve mercy, and African Americans are more likely wish there was a better way than the death penalty. Unpacking this contradictory consciousness in the qualitative analysis further helped to elucidate the contours of black respondents' seemingly conflicting views.

Indeed, if the statistical analysis were taken alone, one would be left with a myriad of possible interpretations for how blacks are confused. Yet rather than simple confusion, black respondents articulate fascinating and complex tales of their sentencing decisions that help us to understand the roots of their contradictory consciousness of law. More specifically, most articulate punitiveness in a traditional model of criminal decision making: they search to find whether the defendant is actually responsible for the crime. Yet, contrary to traditional theories of punishment (Van den Haag 1975), such evaluations are not always so clear-cut—some black respondents' struggled over whether the defendant was guilty of a capital murder. Moreover, evaluating the defendant's criminal responsibility led most respondents (63.6 percent) to question the legitimacy of the legal process ("Every man should pay his own dues") and not always because of their own negative experiences

(36.3 percent) with the criminal justice system. Nevertheless, black jurors' who elaborate on the defendant's responsibility for the crime are more likely to impose the death sentence.

However, punitiveness in other black jurors' stories may be hidden or muffled in descriptions of personal experiences with the crime problem and spiritual transformation. Indeed, the decision to show mercy is a fundamental part of how black respondents' articulate a narrative of moral redemption. Perhaps not surprisingly, given the deep and rich Christian tradition among blacks, especially in the American South (Wilmore 1998), such respondents were found to draw heavily on their religious backgrounds and experiences, which, in turn, informed a search for redeemable qualities in the defendant. But they did not only tell moral redemption stories. Every respondent I investigated expressed some cynicism about the legal system. For Ophelia Street, for example, her deep merciful beliefs were challenged by her own experiences with the crime problem, which, in turn, shaped her cynicism regarding the public financing of the prison system ("You had to be in jail in your own house and pay for them to be in prison").

Prior research has documented variation across social group membership with respect to various paradigms of legal consciousness (Nielsen 2000); however, the analysis presented here demonstrates variation *within* such paradigms. More specifically, while Nielsen's study systematically shows, for example, that respondents of color were more likely than white respondents to oppose legal regulation of offensive speech because they "distrusted authority/were cynical about law" (28 percent versus 7 percent) the data here, albeit in a vastly different context, demonstrate how such distrust of or cynicism about law is mediated by both specifically legal-cynical reasons and by other extralegal issues, such as religious faith.

In short, the consciousness of black capital jurors reveals a complex hegemonic character. Black jurors' stories reveal profound internal contradictions that provide them the ability both to critique and to justify their decisions to impose a life sentence or a death sentence. Conveying a lived marginality experienced personally ("being in jail in your own house") or by the defendant ("having to die for something somebody else did"), black jurors are left to "reconcile the irreconcilable" (Ewick and Silbey 1998, 233). The death penalty as an all-or-nothing decision made in a moral vacuum conceals its decidedly racialized character.

Appendix C
The Jurors

Elizabeth Abbott: female; sentenced to death Elton Bryant, a black unemployed male convicted of murdering Thomas Peller and Matthew Burke, two white male college students.

Mary Albany: female, white, high-school-educated, homemaker; sentenced to life in prison Michael Bishop, a white male who beat to death Devon Wilson, a black male.

Betty Alma: female, white, high-school-educated, homemaker; sentenced to death Pedro Arenas, a Hispanic male who raped and murdered Leslie Royce, a white female.

Avery Anderson: male, white, college-educated, business executive; sentenced to death Arthur Morris, a black male who robbed and murdered Leroy Ivers, a black male.

Dorothy Antonio: female, white, high-school-educated, homemaker; sentenced to life in prison Michael Bishop, a white male who beat to death Devon Wilson, a black male.

Damon Arthur: male, white, college-educated, airline pilot; sentenced to death Pedro Arenas, a Hispanic male who raped and murdered Leslie Royce, a white female.

Candace Ballard: female, white, high-school-educated, secretary; sentenced to death Donald Carson, a white male who raped and murdered Emma Davis (a white female) and shot to death Dwight Davis (a white male), John Davis (a white male), James Davis (a white male), and Thomas Davis (a white male).

Cindy Barlow: female, white, college-educated, schoolteacher; sentenced to death Anson Corliss, a black male who robbed and shot to death a black male, Dwayne Townsend.

Eileen Berg: female, white, college-educated, homemaker; sentenced to death Jesus Elisé, a Hispanic male who murdered Maria Gomez, a Hispanic female.

Henry Berry: male, white, college-educated, business executive; sentenced to death Barry Lawrence, a white male who robbed and shot to death Miguel Pena, a Latino male.

Stuart Brand: male, white, college-educated, schoolteacher; sentenced to death Diego Suarez, a Latino male who murdered Lilly Suarez (Latino female) and Maria Suarez (Latino female).

Sheila Brooks: female, white, college-educated, hairdresser; sentenced to death Ray Floyd Cornish, a black male convicted of shooting Richard Garrett, a white male.

Harold Brown: male, black, high-school-educated, carpenter; sentenced to life in prison Dwayne Whitmore, a black male who killed Dwight Pressey, a black male.

Bart Charles: male, white, high-school-educated, farmer; sentenced to life in prison Joseph Raymond, a black male who murdered Luther Gentry, a black male.

Leanne Croft: female, white, college-educated, health care worker; sentenced to death Cyrus Paxton, a black male who robbed and shot to death Ferguson Brown, a black male.

Stephanie Dambrowski: female, white, high-school-educated, administrative secretary; sentenced to death Stephen Ralphs, a white male who robbed and shot to death Gerry Trent, a white male.

Fred Dawson: male, white, college-educated, business executive; sentenced to death Devon Wiggins, a black male convicted of shooting George Walker, a white male.

Florence Delbert: female, white, high-school-educated, retired salesperson; sentenced to death Jesus Elisé, a Hispanic male who murdered Maria Gomez, a Hispanic female.

Frank Dod: male, white, high-school-educated, plumber; sentenced to death Alfred Watson, a black male who shot to death Jerome Hampton, a black male.

Pamela Drake: female, white, college-educated, homemaker; sentenced to life in prison Joseph Raymond, a black male who murdered Luther Gentry, a black male.

Wayne Fenwick: male, white, college-educated, middle-class businessman; sentenced to life in prison Kenneth Yardley, a white male who raped and murdered Charlene Fergus, a white female.

Ronald Fredrickson: male, auto mechanic; sentenced to life in prison (but was overridden by a pro-death majority) Arthur Chester, a black male convicted of murdering Michael Simpkins, a white male police officer.

Bernadette Garvin: female, white, college-educated, homemaker; sentenced to life without parole Lawrence Kendrick, a white male who beat to death Thomas Winter, a white male.

David Granger: male, black, college-educated, attorney; sentenced to life in prison Morris Green, a black male who murdered Sean Ray, a white male.

Stan Harris: male, white, graduate-school-educated, software engineer; sentenced to death Jesus Elisé, a Hispanic male who murdered Maria Gomez, a Hispanic female.

Anne Hernandez: female, high-school-educated, secretary; sentenced to death Clayton Wallace, a white male who raped and murdered Roberta Stuckey, a white female.

Terry Jansen: female, white, college-educated, real estate agent; sentenced to death Diego Suarez, a Latino male who murdered Lilly Suarez (Latino female) and Maria Suarez (Latino female).

Colleen Kirk: female, white, high-school-educated, social worker; sentenced to life in prison David Gomez, a white male who robbed and murdered Frank Grenadier, a white male.

Madeline Kraft: female, white, college-educated, financial consultant; sentenced to death Stephen Ralphs, a white male who robbed and shot to death Gerry Trent, a white male.

Ralph Lewis: male, white, high-school-educated, retired farmer; sentenced to death Alfred Watson, a black male who shot to death Jerome Hampton, a black male.

Sherman Lewis: male, white, college-educated, industrial plant manager; sentenced to death Anthony Finch, a white male who robbed and murdered Earl Jennings, a white male, and Sandra Jennings, a white female.

Howard Lively: male, white, high-school-educated, construction supervisor; sentenced to death Warren Brown, a white male who shot to death Laura and Melissa Hildebrand, white.

Shirley Loman: female, white, high-school-educated, secretary; sentenced to death Gary White, a black male who robbed and shot to death Barbara Anders, a white female.

Gary Lombardo: male, white, college-educated, filmmaker; sentenced to life in prison Morris Green, a black male who murdered Sean Ray, a white male.

Deidre Lund: female, white, high-school-educated, sales representative; sentenced to death Tommy Struthers, a black male who robbed and murdered Troy Kingston, a black male.

Georgette Madison: female, white, college-educated, intensive-care-nursery health care practitioner; sentenced to death Barry Lawrence, a white male who robbed and shot to death Miguel Pena, a Latino male.

Barrett Mannheim: male, white, college-educated, schoolteacher; sentenced to life in prison Morris Green, a black male who murdered Sean Ray, a white male.

Bonnie Mayer: female, white, high-school-educated, homemaker; sentenced to death Cal Swenson, a white male who raped and strangled to death a white female, Ruth Parsons.

Nancy McAdams: female, white, high-school-educated, secretary; sentenced to life in prison Mark Jarvis, a black male who shot to death Richard Jackson (black male) and Quinten Harris (black male).

Sandy McClintock: female, white, college-educated, sales manager; sentenced to death Barry Lawrence, a white male who robbed and shot to death Miguel Pena, a Latino male.

Dexter Megget: male, black, high-school-educated, construction worker; sentenced to life in prison Toby Leeson, a black male who shot to death Roy Vincent, a white male police officer.

Wanda Nelson: female, white, high-school-educated, homemaker; sentenced to life in prison Michael Sanchez, a Latino male who, along with four accomplices, murdered three black males, Michael Esterdige, Rayford Savoy, and Anthony Pallance.

Wayne Nickerson: male, graduate-school-educated, mechanical engineer; sentenced to death Gary White, a black male who robbed and shot to death Barbara Anders, a white female.

Leslie Odom: female, white, high-school-educated, homemaker; sentenced to death Derek Tanner, a white male who raped and murdered a white female, Louise Miller.

Ruth Randolph: female, black, high-school-educated, administrative assistant; sentenced to death Ivan Strayhorn, a black male who robbed and murdered Ruth Grier, a black female.

Albert Reynolds: male, white, high-school-educated, mechanic; sentenced to death Barry Lawrence, a white male who robbed and shot to death Miguel Pena, a Latino male.

Walter Robertson: male, white, college-educated, financial manager; sentenced to death Luis Rodriguez, a Latino male who robbed and shot to death Francis Salvo, a Latino male.

Jessie Salvi: male, high-school-educated, sales manager; sentenced to death Clayton Wallace, a white male who raped and murdered Roberta Stuckey, a white female.

Cindy Sanford: female, white, college-educated, homemaker; sentenced to life in prison Mark Jarvis, a black male who shot to death Richard Jackson (black male) and Quinten Harris (black male).

Gail Scuttles: female, white, high-school-educated, homemaker; sentenced to death Gary White, a black male who robbed and shot to death Barbara Anders, a white female.

Melvin Seagal: male, white, college-educated, retired social worker; sentenced to death Frank Sharpe, an African American male who shot to death Ralph Sharpe, a black male.

Shirley Sharpe: female, black, college-educated, secretary; sentenced to death Earl Winston, a black male who robbed and shot to death Joshua Hall, a white male.

Angela Stephens: female, white, college-educated, sales manager; sentenced to life in prison Michael Bishop, a white male who beat to death Devon Wilson, a black male.

Ophelia Street: female, black, high-school-educated, seamstress; sentenced to life in prison Morris Sanford, a black male who shot to death Rashanda Clement, a black female.

Robert Waingrow: male, white, high-school-educated, construction worker; sentenced to death Ivan Strayhorn, a black male who robbed and murdered Ruth Grier, a black female.

Molly Wegler: female, white, administrative assistant; sentenced to death Diego Suarez, a Latino male who murdered Lilly Suarez, a Latino female, and Maria Suarez, a Latino female.

Margaret Wentworth: female, white, college-educated, high school teacher; sentenced to death Donald Carson, a white male who raped and murdered Emma Davis (a white female) and shot to death Dwight Davis (a white male), John Davis (a white male), James Davis (a white male), and Thomas Davis (a white male).

Theodore Willis: male, truck driver; sentenced to death Thomas Frank, a white male convicted of murdering his parents John and Delores Frank and his brother Lewis Frank.

Lynette Worrell: female, white, high-school-educated, former youth counselor; sentenced to death Pedro Arenas, a Hispanic male who raped and murdered Leslie Royce, a white female.

Notes

Chapter 1

1. Throughout this book I use terms such as *state-sanctioned punishment* and *state enlistees* (for jurors). My use of the term *state* refers explicitly to the legislatures that have made the punishment of death a legally enforceable policy, to the prosecuting officials who act on these laws, and to the courts that uphold and thus legitimize the imposition of the death penalty in practice. Where does this leave the twelve citizens who make life-or-death decisions? *Jurors' Stories of Death* presents an answer to this question: laypersons are acting under the coercion of state-mandated jury service and thus must be seen as making the awesome life-or-death decision under institutionalized duress.

My presentation of jurors' stories gives voice to the laypersons whom the state orders to decide whether to take a life. To be sure, jurors' stories present a window into state-sanctioned death as punishment, but they do not represent the voices of those most responsible for the continued use of capital punishment in America today. As will be come clearer in the chapters that follow, jurors' stories paint a vivid portrait of a nation that continues to struggle with its racist past. Yet such voices can be heard as legal only in the context of the broader state institutions that implement, enforce, and defend death as punishment. As will be shown, jurors' stories are often complex voices of anger, contradiction, and fear. They typically are not, as the state would have one presume, cold and calculated tales of retributive justice.

2. To preserve jurors' anonymity, throughout this book I have used pseudonyms in place of actual names. I have also changed various factual details surrounding cases whenever I was concerned that certain issues might jeopardize anonymity.

3. "The story of the oppression of blacks by force has been told in literally hundreds of reports, histories, narratives and studies" (Bell 1974, 857; see also Kennedy 1997).

4. As will become apparent, jurors' stories are replete with variations on the theme of individual responsibility. "The notion that people freely 'choose' crime derives, in part, from the notion that people are responsible

for their own welfare (self-reliance), and in part from the veneration people attach to the act of choosing (individualism)" (Sasson 1995, 150).

5. "The lives of many capital defendants are bereft of the things we now know are essential to normal psychological development—'dependable attachment, protection, guidance, stimulation, nurturance, and ways of coping with adversity.' . . . Instead, they often confront the multiple risk factors of poverty, chronic neglect, emotional and physical abuse, and extreme familial instability with little to buffer them from the predictable harm" (Haney 1998, 364).

6. "In capital cases, prospective jurors' death-qualification status . . . serves as the basis for a challenge of cause: an attorney will challenge for cause any prospective juror he or she believes would not follow the law in determining the appropriate sentence" (Sandys 1998, 286).

7. However, the current Supreme Court has placed less of an emphasis on how jurors employ such sentencing instructions. For a review of these cases, see Steiker and Steiker 1998.

8. I thank Jack Katz for helping me to clarify my thesis.

Chapter 2

1. Adapted from *McCleskey v. Kemp* 481 U.S. 279 (1987).

2. "The civil rights revolution came to a standstill in the 1980s, and many African Americans now believe that the country and its government are moving backward in the quest for racial justice. Presidential use of the 'bully pulpit' for conservative political agendas during the Reagan and Bush years of the 1980s and early 1990s was particularly devastating to racial relations. Federal civil rights enforcement programs were weakened significantly in this period. The political denial of white racism made its way into intellectual circles and the mass media, where the concept of the 'declining significance of race' became fashionable" (Feagin and Vera 1995, 3).

3. For a discussion of how gender was racialized in political storytelling in the war on drugs, see Steiner 2001.

4. "The final version of the Violent Crime Control and Law Enforcement Act of 1994 authorized $6.9 billion for crime prevention efforts, $13.8 billion for law enforcement, and $9.8 billion for state prison construction. . . . The legislation also created dozens of new federal capital crimes, mandated life sentences for some three-time offenders, restricted the scope of court-ordered settlements in lawsuits seeking improved prison conditions. . . . The legislation was sent to President Clinton in August 1994 and was hailed as a victory for the Democrats, who 'were able to wrest the crime issue from the Republicans and make it their own'" (Beckett and Sasson 2000, 72).

5. Both President Clinton and Attorney General Janet Reno opposed Senator Russell Feingold's (D-Wisconsin) proposal for a national death penalty moratorium (see "Color of Skin" 2000, A14).

6. I thank Alex Sugarman-Brozan for his insight on this point.

7. The critical race project focuses on deconstructing the black-white binary implicit in the racialized narratives of crime and punishment in the contemporary United States. Challenging traditional legal categories as amorphous and, most importantly, capable of normalizing identities, scholars such as Crenshaw (1995) have called attention to the "intersectionality" of race and gender identities:

> Identities inter-exist, each inseparable, depending on the other and practically indistinguishable. The black woman's blackness is brought into being by her femininity and, conversely, her femininity is defined and realized in and through her blackness. . . . In other words, there is no "choose faces" because the only one who exists does so in and through the very identity categories it is said to be outside. Thus we are already identified through discourse and language. (Oberweis and Musheno 2001, 56)

While this project has been invaluable for reconceptualizing research on identity, the study of intersectionality has been met with some important criticisms.

First, sexual orientation (Goldberg-Hiller 2002) and class (Robson 1995) are invariably excluded from such analyses. Moreover, critics have observed that by privileging race and gender identities, the theory risks reproducing "social marginalization at the analytical level by shaping new quasi-essentialist categories such as 'black women' or by simplifying social relations in binary terms of black/white as the central paradigm of race" (Goldberg-Hiller 2002, 185). However, recent research on the Latino/a experience (Gomez 1998; Montoya 1998) provides an important corrective. By situating racial hierarchy in the broader contexts of history and institutional constraints, this scholarship presents a more nuanced critique of how

> narratives instantiate power to the degree that they regulate silence and colonize consciousness. . . . As subversive stories . . . they are capable of countering the hegemonic . . . without denying the particularities of experience and subjectivities and those which bear witness to what is unimagined and unexpressed. (Ewick and Silbey 1995, 220)

8. For a fascinating genealogical analysis of abortion rhetoric, see Condit 1994.

9. See chaps. 4–8 for further elaboration on the story of individual responsibility.

10. Ethnographic research finds that a so-called breakdown in morality is a prominent theme in citizens' "crime talk" (Sasson 1995). As discussions between two focus group members illustrates (Beckett and Sasson 2000, 137–38),

> GLORIA: I feel as though [crime is] happening because of the homes that some of these young people may come out of. Lack of supervision, lack of parents—parents being parents.
>
> BEN: No guidance. ["Right!"—a voice interjects.] A few years back on TV, you remember, "It's 11:00 o'clock, do you know where your children are?" And the answer to that today is, "Yeah, they're outside on the street somewhere."
>
> GLORIA: No commitment in the home, no commitment in schools. Parents do not go to parent-teacher meetings. They don't go to the schools until the student has a real serious problem.
>
> BEN: And then they get angry at the teacher.
>
> GLORIA: Yes. Or angry with the principal, or angry with the guidance counselor, or angry with the bus drivers. It's everybody else's fault.
>
> BEN: There is no respect.

11. Perhaps Justice Scalia's most notorious statement of his punishment-at-all-costs jurisprudence was revealed not in a legal decision but in a memo he circulated to Justice Lewis Powell prior to the Court's *McCleskey* decision.

> Scalia's memo, dated January 6 . . . did understand the power of Baldus's numbers, and he was obviously troubled by the statistical know-nothingness of Powell's opinion. But the bottom line for McCleskey was no different. In Scalia's view, Powell had pinned too much on wrongly alleged weaknesses in the Baldus study, as if a better statistical showing might have carried the day. "Since it is my view," [Scalia] wrote, "that the unconscious operation of irrational sympathies and antipathies, including racial, upon jury decisions and (hence) prosecutorial decisions is real, acknowledged in the decisions of this court, and ineradicable, I cannot honestly say that all I need is more proof." In other words, Scalia basically agreed . . . that some racial bias in capital sentencing was inevitable. He was, however, willing to tolerate that bias and even thought that the other Justices, in candor, should admit they were too. (Lazarus 1998, 211)

12. "A great many capital jurors do not remain impartial about punishment until the penalty phase of the trial and nevertheless serve as capital jurors" (Bowers, Sandys, and Steiner 1998, 1537).

13. Furthermore, an imposing collection of studies on racialized stereotypes (Barkan and Cohn 1994; Sweeney and Haney 1992) and racialized fears of crime find increased punitiveness among whites (Sunnafrank and Fontes 1983). Like blacks, Hispanics are also disproportionately perceived as aggressive, uneducated, poor, and more prone to violence (for a review, see Castro 1998). Moreover, those who hold such negative stereotypes are found to live in predominantly suburban areas segregated from the Hispanic community (Marín 1984).

Other studies document links between racial stereotypes and punishment for specific crimes. Indeed, studies demonstrate that white respondents presented with vignettes of violent crimes committed by black offenders yield stronger correlations between race and punitiveness than more diffuse indicators of crime and punitiveness.

> Racial stereotypes [are] only modestly correlated with attitudes toward generic crime issues [e.g., the death penalty], our punitiveness and civil liberties scales, and so on. . . . The conditional impact of race, however, in no way minimizes its importance. Violent crimes committed by blacks, and the policies designed to punish them, are the very images which drive public fears. . . . They are conflated by the media, by individuals like Charles Stewart and Susan Smith (both of whom blamed African American males for crimes they, themselves, committed), and by cynical political messengers who "Willie Hortonize" campaigns. (Hurwitz and Peffley 1997, 395–96; see also Hurwitz and Peffley 1998)

Thus, we might expect former capital jurors to employ similar racialized discourses in their stories of making their sentencing decisions.

14. As Franklin D. Gilliam observes, "During the election Reagan often recited the story of a woman from Chicago's South Side who was arrested for welfare fraud:

> She has 80 names, 30 addresses, 12 Social Security cards and is collecting veteran's benefits on four non-existing deceased husbands. And she is collecting Social Security on her cards. She's got Medicaid, getting food stamps, and she is collecting welfare under each of her names.

The implicit racial coding is readily apparent. The woman Reagan was talking about was African American. Veiled references to African American
women, and African Americans in general, were equally transparent. In
other words, while poor women of all races get blamed for their impoverished condition, African American women commit the most egregious vio-
lations of American values. This story line taps into stereotypes about both
women (uncontrolled sexuality) and African Americans (laziness)" (Gilliam
1999).

15. "White workers found themselves competing with low-paid Chinese
workers for scarce jobs and viewed the Chinese as an economic threat. The
campaign against *smoking* opium (but not against other, non-Chinese uses
of opiates) included lurid, fictional newspaper accusations of Chinese men
drugging white women into sexual slavery" (Reinarman and Levine 1997,
6–7). In his insightful analysis of early American drug wars, historian David
Musto (1973) demonstrates that cocaine policies targeting blacks were less
concerned with health issues and more with the subordination and control
of such racially defined groups.

16. By incorporating the political, cultural, and bureaucratic insights
highlighted in this chapter as a central feature of my analysis, I traveled two
methodological paths. The most pronounced was the subjective road of
interpreting jurors' experiences as capital jurors. While I will discuss this in
more detail in the next chapter, I clearly privilege how jurors' "experienced
meaning instead of their overt actions or behavior" (Riessman 1994, xiv).
However, the more I noticed the often contradictory and conflicting voices
in jurors' stories, the more I realized that I needed to explore jurors'
broader attitudes and beliefs (see appendix B). Yet this turn did not lead me
into the ontological wilderness (although I thought at times that it would).
To the contrary, the statistical analysis heightened my sense of the complexity of jurors' stories. Using quantitative approaches (see appendix B), I
in effect gained insights that enriched my phenomenological analysis of
jurors' stories. In the next chapter, I discuss this methodological process in
greater detail.

Chapter 3

1. While the sentencing of women to death has been a growing trend in
recent years, none of the cases I present here involve female defendants
(e.g., Death Penalty Information Center 2002); thus, I refer to offenders in
the masculine.

2. Quantitative methods have, however, been helpful to me in gaining a
better sense of the African American jurors (see appendix B). Thus, I believe
it is not sufficient to say that narrative methods answer the questions
addressed in this book "better" than other methods. To the contrary, I

believe that the statistical tables presented in appendix B helped me to frame the analysis. More specifically, because the narrative material lends itself to an examination of each broad substantive theme—how the insiders differ from the resisters—readers may have the tendency to believe that these types of capital jurors can somehow be broken into clean dichotomies. Focusing on African American jurors, as I do in appendix B, reveals that a disproportionate number of them tell stories of resistance; consequently, readers may be led erroneously to construct the insider-resister split as a clean racial dichotomy (blacks are resisters and whites are insiders). Yet a closer analysis of African American jurors' attitudes and beliefs regarding crime and the criminal justice process reveals that their consciousness is far more complex. As will become evident, elucidating such complexities in the statistical tables lends important clarity to my analysis of the stories of black and white jurors from the same case (see chap. 7).

3. For a detailed review of how states were selected according to state statutory guidelines, see Bowers 1995, 1077–80.

4. The Capital Jury Project data include 24 trials represented by five jurors, 8 by six jurors, and 1 by eight jurors. Unfortunately, in some instances, despite a twenty-dollar incentive, jurors refused to be interviewed. More specifically, 39 trials are represented by a single juror, 45 by two jurors, 71 by three, 152 by four, 31 by five, 13 by six, 1 by seven, and 1 by eight jurors.

5. As demonstrated in previous analyses of the CJP data (Bowers, Steiner, and Sandys 2001; Fleury-Steiner 2002) the issue of race and how it was represented in jurors' stories has been of primary importance to CJP investigators. Indeed, this book is in many ways both an elaboration and an expansion of that previous work. Specifically, seven of the eight from a previous analysis of jurors' race in death cases (e.g., Fleury-Steiner 2001) are examined in more detail here. They are Sheila Brooks, Melvin Seagal, Robert Waingrow, Ralph Lewis, Fred Dawson, Ronald Fredrickson, and Shirley Sharpe. The present work expands the reach of that earlier research to a wider sample of jurors including Latino and marginal white defendants as well as life cases.

6. "Something of Nietzsche's mountain-top air of transvaluation clings to the tragic hero: His thoughts are not any more than his deeds, even if, like Faustus, he is dragged off to hell for having them. . . . Tragedy seems to lead up to an epiphany of law, of that which is and must be" (Frye 1957, 207–8).

7. While the conservative backlash against judicial activism began as a response to the Warren Court's sweeping activist jurisprudence of the 1950s and 1960s, this rhetoric continues to thrive in modern politics (see, e.g., Wolfe 1991).

Chapter 4

1. While in a previous study (Fleury-Steiner 2002) I indicated that Fred Dawson served on the Cornish jury, I later learned that both Cornish and Wiggins were accomplices in the same crime, but tried separately. Fred Dawson was a juror in the Wiggins case.

2. "The site of revenge has increasingly become the law in an attempt to pry courts and legal doctrines loose from the demands of lesbians and gays and from the sovereign imaginary across a broad spectrum of issues. Service in the military, criminal regulation of same-sex conduct, employment protections against discriminatory treatment and same-sex harassment, public speech and the right to parade, domestic partnership and same-sex marriage have all been sites of intense anti–gay rights politics" (Goldberg-Hiller 2002, 17).

3. In the context of crime, the media have created the illusion of African and Latin American criminality at the same time that they have created the illusion of white innocence. Thus, in his analysis of more than thirty-five years of crime coverage in American newsmagazines, Robert Elias observes,

> blacks and other non-white minorities were described and pictured in the newsweeklies' crime coverage most frequently even though these groups *do not* commit the majority of crimes. . . . In contrast, the newsweeklies described and pictured victims mostly as white people. What emerges from my study is a pattern of discrimination in which criminals are conceptualized as [people of color] and crime as the violence they do to whites. (1994, 5)

While the vast majority of violent crime is intraracial (see Walker, Spohn, and DeLone 2000), the media construct crime as a white victimization problem at that same time that they construct it as an African and Latin American criminality problem.

Chapter 5

1. "In the Philadelphia system, prosecutors appear to have been guided by a model outlined in a 1986 video training tape for Philadelphia prosecutors prepared by then-homicide prosecutor Jack M. It emphasizes the importance of voir dire and the overarching goal of seating jurors who are 'conviction-prone,' possess a good respect for 'law [and] authority,' are predisposed to accept the government's claims at face value, and are 'more likely to convict than anybody else in that room.' M also identifies the jurors to be avoided as those who 'inherently may be against the govern-

ment or against police or against the Commonwealth in some way, shape, or form'" (Baldus et al. 2001, 41–42).

2. To reconstruct this crime, I drew on trial transcripts whenever available, court opinions, news reports, and the jurors' interviews. To preserve the defendant's anonymity, I use pseudonyms for all relevant individuals, and I have slightly modified the case's factual content. At my own discretion, I have made minor changes to factual details so as to protect jurors' anonymity.

3. "The language suggests that someone subordinated under one form of oppression would be similarly situated to another person subordinated under another form" (Wildman 1996, 12).

Chapter 6

1. To preserve anonymity to all parties, I use pseudonyms and have changed factual information whenever appropriate.

2. Approximately 42.9 percent of all black males and 57.1 percent of all black females who served on black defendant–black victim cases served on juries with at least four other black jurors (Bowers, Sandys, and Steiner 2001, 192).

3. Writing about the cultural messages embedded in the Rodney King incident, Thomas L. Dumm observes, "In the American version of normalized society, the least normal (and most despised) group of people are young black men" (1993, 178).

4. Jurors were asked at about their stands on punishment (1) after the guilt stage of the trial; (2) after the judge's sentencing instructions to the jury but before the jury's deliberations regarding punishment; (3) at the jury's first vote on punishment; and (4) at the jury's final vote on punishment.

5. Closely following Oberweis and Musheno (2001), I evaluated jurors' stories "as sites of legal practice, searching for valuative content of these moments while freeing [myself] from the presuppositions that formal law is or should be the normative guide of these practices" (7).

6. It was not clear in either the court opinions or in jurors' interviews what White was using the money for.

7. This is analogous to what Joe R. Feagin and Hernán Vera (1995, 138–41), in their important study of white racism, call a "white bubble." As one of their respondents illustrates,

In the past three years, we are suddenly having robberies that have never happened before. We are one of two houses on the street that have not been hit. . . . The man across the street has theorized that a bunch of lowlifes have moved in into a local government housing area. I don't know where it's coming from, but I think it's flashed through every mind that it's probably blacks, including mine. And I'm so ashamed of that. I immediately shake myself and say, "No, it isn't." [Where do you suppose that feeling comes from?] Society. You hear it all the time. I think it gets grilled into us. (153)

Chapter 7

1. Further information regarding Elisé's background was not readily available in public records or from other sources.

2. "The growth and transformation of [the] underclass is in large part a result of profound economic changes the country . . . has undergone in the past twenty years to thirty years. Deindustrialization and the growth of the global economy have led to a steady loss of the unskilled and semiskilled manufacturing jobs that, with mixed results, had sustained the urban working class since the start of the industrial revolution" (Anderson 2000, 108; see also Wilson 1987, 1997).

3. In many respects, these stories represent an interesting variation on the caring family. While these jurors declare that the foreign man is not one of them, they are sympathetic to his cultural predicament. As a paternalistic discourse, these stories deny the possibility that the insiders and the foreign resister could ever be "systematically opposed in an antagonistic relationship" (Du Toit 1993, 321). To the contrary, they represent the foreign man as both helpless and adversarial. Or, to put it another way, he could not possibly understand broken justice—he is not from around here.

4. "Gender differences, or the sociocultural shaping of the 'essential female and male natures,' achieve the status of objective facts. They are rendered normal, natural features of persons and provide the tacit rationale for differing fates of women and men within the social order" (West and Zimmerman 1987, 142).

5. "In this light, the institutional arrangements of a society can be seen as responsive to the differences—the social order being merely an accommodation of the natural order. Thus if, in doing gender, men are also doing dominance and women are doing deference, the resultant social order, which supposedly reflects 'natural differences,' is a powerful reinforcer and legitimator of hierarchical arrangements" (West and Zimmerman 1987, 146).

Chapter 8

1. "This unusual degree of segregation is largely involuntary and stems from the operation of three interrelated and mutually reinforcing forces in

American society: high levels of institutionalized discrimination in the real estate and banking industries; high levels of prejudice among whites against blacks as potential neighbors; and discriminatory public policies implemented by whites at all levels of government. Racial segregation is not simply a historical legacy of past prejudice and discrimination. On the contrary, it is actively perpetuated by institutional actions, private behaviors, and public policies that continue to the present day" (Massey 1995, 1227).

2. Criminal justice reform alone obviously is a limited site for a progressive politics of resistance. Any real change will depend on an activist agenda and philanthropic base not unlike the step program outlined by the San Francisco Bay Area Committee for Responsive Philanthropy in the 1970s:

(1) Working for a fairer distribution of income or wealth; or (2) working for increased social or political empowerment of oppressed people, especially among racial minorities, women, sexual minorities, the elderly, the handicapped, youth, working class or poor; or (3) working to meet the immediate survival needs of oppressed people. (Rabinowitz 1990, 14)

3. The rhetoric of death penalty reform focuses on "fixing" the capital punishment protocol, especially greater access to DNA testing for convicted capital offenders. While mistaken identification is the most common way an individual is wrongfully convicted (Scheck, Neufeld, and Dwyer 2000), DNA has been presented as a "silver bullet" in reformist arguments. Indeed, even death penalty proponents have recently used DNA as grounds for strengthening death penalty support. In a *St. Louis Post-Dispatch* article, Alexander Tabbarok, the director of the Independent Foundation, a policy think tank that, perhaps not surprisingly, is heavily supported by the biogenetic industry, wrote,

More often than not, genetic testing proves beyond a shadow of a doubt that a prisoner is guilty. . . . As time wears on there will be fewer and fewer "old" cases that can benefit from DNA technology. . . . In the long run, the real impact of genetic testing will surely be to increase, not decrease, support for the death penalty. (Tabbarok and Helland 2000, B7)

4. "The language of international human rights not only captured the prior repression, but also offered a means to inspire and galvanize a liberal opposition as well as an image of hope. Here the language of rights shapes that of political discourse. The claim of rights convergent with that of poli-

tics demand promises mediating differences of culture, and building such discourse promises solidarity among diverse peoples. Ultimately, deliberations are thought to enable gradual consensus. At the very least, the rights practices instantiate those of democracy" (Teitel 1997, 317).

Appendix A

1. Ewick and Silbey (1995, 220) identify three characteristics that may facilitate the rise of what they call "subversive stories": the outsiders (1) are socially marginal in that "their lives and experiences are least likely to find to find expression" in the hegemonic story of the insiders; (2) understand the insiders' master narrative and know its overriding agenda; and (3) are the product of an institution that fosters "both a common opportunity to narrate and a common content to the narrative, thus revealing the collective organization in personal life."

Appendix B

1. Throughout this appendix, my use of the term *legal consciousness* closely mirrors Nielsen's explanation.

> Legal consciousness research examines the role of law (broadly conceived) and its role in constructing understandings, affecting actions, and shaping various aspects of social life. It centers on the study of individuals' experiences with law and legal norms, decisions about legal compliance, and a detailed exploration of the subtle ways in which law affects the everyday lives of individuals to articulate the various understandings of law/legality that people have and use to construct their understanding of their world. (2000, 1059)

2. Haney, Hurtado, and Vega's (1994) study of 498 California respondents' death penalty attitudes found that "modern" death qualification continues to produce a group of eligible jurors that is significantly more punitive than those eligible to sit in any other type of criminal case.

3. Darlington, Weinberg, and Walberg (1973) have summarized a typical factor analysis as shedding light on four interrelated questions: (1) How many different factors are needed to explain the pattern of relationships among these variables? (2) What is the nature of those factors? (3) How well do the hypothesized factors explain the observed data? (4) How much purely random or unique variance does each observed variable include? In this way and in this analysis, factor analysis yields scores for various related dependent variables that may be combined into indexes.

4. In factor analyses of the eighteen statements in the survey, two groupings emerged as distinct factors consisting of the same items in each of the
three samples. This table shows the factor loadings after orthogonal Varimax rotation. Both indexes are scored on a four-point metric: Strong = 1;
Moderate = 2; Low = 3; No Answer (N/A) = 4.

Factor Loadings after Orthogonal Varimax Rotation (Statements 1–18)*

Item	Factors	
	1	2
1	.317	.369
2	.376	.543
3	.369	.441
4	.692	.011
5	.397	.157
6	.324	.503
7	.724	.111
8	.696	.146
9	.748	.256
10	.304	.517
11	.383	.272
12	.679	.364
13	.274	.148
14	.633	.397
15	.411	.270
16	.689	.386
17	.276	.606
18	.435	.182

*Factors in the component matrix that did not yield groupings are not
shown.

5. To test the null hypothesis that race is not related to cynical/pro-
defendant attitudes, I conducted Guttman's coefficient of predictability (λ).
Findings indicated a λ of .133 (white = 1; black = 2) that was significant at
.011. Thus, the null hypothesis can be rejected, and the research hypothesis
that blacks are more cynical/pro-defendant than whites are can be accepted.

6. To accurately locate jurors who were strong (scored 1) on both the
punitive/pro-victim and the cynical/pro-defendant indexes, all "no answers
(N/A)" were eliminated prior to the construction of the contradictory-con-
sciousness index.

7. While there are obvious similarities, my use of the criminal-responsi-

bility narrative presented here implies a more specific articulation of the defendant's actions relative to the insiders' story of individual responsibility (see chap. 4), which I use to highlight a more diffuse cultural logic of pulling oneself up by the bootstraps.

8. For evidence of lingering doubt among black jurors in the Capital Jury Project more broadly, see Bowers, Sandys, and Steiner 2001.

9. Despite being torn between prison's effectiveness at facilitating the defendant's moral redemption, the majority (60 percent) of black jurors articulating such a narrative served on juries that imposed life sentences (see table B4).

Bibliography

Alcoff, Linda. 1988. "Cultural Feminism Versus Post-Structuralism: The Identity Crisis in Feminist Theory." *Signs* 13:405–31.

Anderson, Elijah. 1992. *Streetwise: Race, Class, and Change in an Urban Community*. Chicago: University of Chicago Press.

———. 2000. *Code of the Street: Decency, Violence, and the Moral Life of the Inner City*. New York: W. W. Norton.

Anspach, Renée R. 1993. *Deciding Who Lives: Fateful Choices in the Intensive-Care Nursery*. Berkeley: University of California Press.

Bailey, F. G. 1983. *The Tactical Uses of Passion*. Ithaca: Cornell University Press.

Baldus, David C., George Woodworth, and Charles Pulaski Jr. 1990. *Equal Justice and the Death Penalty: A Legal and Empirical Analysis*. Boston: Northeastern University Press.

Baldus, David C., George Woodworth, David Zuckerman, Neil Alan Weiner, and Barbara Broffitt. 2001. "The Use of Peremptory Challenges in Capital Murder Trials: A Legal and Empirical Analysis." *Pennsylvania Journal of Constitutional Law* 3:3–170.

Barkan, Steven E., and Steven F. Cohn. 1994. "Prejudice and Support for the Death Penalty by Whites." *Journal of Research in Crime and Delinquency* 31:202–9.

Beckett, Katherine. 1997. *Making Crime Pay: Law and Order in Contemporary American Politics*. New York: Oxford University Press.

Beckett, Katherine, and Theodore Sasson. 2000. *The Politics of Injustice: Crime and Punishment in America*. Thousand Oaks, CA: Pine Forge Press.

Bell, Derek A., Jr. 1974. *Race, Racism, and American Law*. Boston: Little, Brown.

———. 1987. *And We Are Not Saved: The Elusive Quest for Racial Justice*. New York: Basic Books.

Bennett, W. Lance, and Martha S. Feldman. 1981. *Reconstructing Reality in the Courtroom: Justice and Judgment in American Culture*. Piscataway, NJ: Rutgers University Press.

Bentele, Ursula. 1998. "Back to an International Perspective on the Death Penalty as a Cruel Punishment: The Example of South Africa." *Tulane Law Review* 73:251–304.

Bentele, Ursula, and William J. Bowers. 2001. "How Jurors Decide on Death: Guilt Is Overwhelming, Aggravation Requires Death, and Mitigation Is No Excuse." *Brooklyn Law Review* 66:1001–80.

Borg, Marian J. 1998. "Vicarious Homicide Victimization and Support for Capital Punishment: A Test of Black's Theory of Law." *Criminology* 36:537–67.

Bourgois, Philippe. 1996. *In Search of Respect: Selling Crack in El Barrio.* New York: Cambridge University Press.

Bowers, William J. 1995. "The Capital Jury Project: Rationale, Design, and a Preview of Early Findings." *Indiana Law Journal* 70:1043–1102.

Bowers, William J., Marla Sandys, and Benjamin D. Steiner. 1998. "Foreclosed Impartiality in Capital Sentencing: Jurors' Predispositions, Guilt-Trial Experience, and Premature Punishment Decision Making." *Cornell Law Review* 83:1476–1556.

———. 2001. "Death Sentencing in Black and White: An Empirical Examination of Juror Race and Jury Racial Composition in Capital Sentencing." *Pennsylvania Journal of Constitutional Law* 3:171–274.

Bowers, William J., and Benjamin D. Steiner. 1998. "Choosing Life or Death: Sentencing Dynamics in Capital Cases." In *America's Experiment with Capital Punishment,* ed. James R. Acker, Robert M. Bohm, and Charles S. Lanier. Durham, NC: Carolina Academic Press.

———. 1999. "Death by Default: An Empirical Demonstration of Forced and False Choices in Capital Sentencing." *University of Texas Law Review* 77:608–717.

Bush, George H. W. 1989. "Remarks at the Acres Homes War on Drugs Rally in Houston, Texas." In *Public Papers of the Presidents 1989,* vol. 2. Washington, DC: U.S. Government Printing Office.

Butler, Paul. 1997. "Affirmative Action and the Criminal Law." *University of Colorado Law Review* 68:841–89.

Carbado, Devon W. 1999. *Black Men on Race, Gender, and Sexuality: A Critical Reader.* New York: New York University Press.

Castro, Diego O. 1998. "'Hot Blood and Easy Virtue': Mass Media and the Making of Latino/a Stereotypes." In *Images of Color, Images of Crime,* ed. Coramae Richey Mann and Marjorie S. Zatz. Los Angeles: Roxbury.

Chomet, Julian. 1990. *Speed and Amphetamines.* New York: F. Watts.

Cole, David. 1999. *No Equal Justice: Race and Class in the American Criminal Justice System.* New York: New Press.

Cole, Melissa. 1999. "The Color-Blind Constitution, Civil Rights-Talk, and a Multicultural Discourse for a Post-Reparations World." *New York University Review of Law and Social Change* 25:127–80.

Condit, Celeste Michelle. 1994. *Decoding Abortion Rhetoric: Communicating Social Change.* Urbana: University of Illinois Press.

Crenshaw, Kimberlé. 1995. "Mapping the Margins: Intersectionality, Identity Politics, and Violence against Women." In *After Identity: A Reader in Law and Culture,* ed. Dan Danielsen and Karen Engle. New York: Routledge.

———. 1997. "Color-Blind Dreams and Racial Nightmares: Reconfiguring Racism in the Post–Civil Rights Era." In *Birth of a Nation 'Hood: Gaze, Script, and Spectacle in the O. J. Simpson Case,* ed. Toni Morrison and Claudia Bronsky Lacour. New York: Pantheon.

Crenshaw, Kimberlé, N. Gotanda, G. Peller, and K. Thomas. 1996. *Critical Race Theory: The Key Writings That Formed the Movement.* New York: New Press.

Darlington, R. B., S. Weinberg, and H. Walberg. 1973. "Canonical Variate Analysis and Related Techniques." *Review of Educational Research* 43:433–54.

Davis, Angela Y. 1978. "Rape, Racism, and the Capitalist Setting." *Black Scholar* 9 (7): 24–30.

Death Penalty Information Center. 2002. "Death Row USA Summer 2002, as of July 1, 2002." www.deathpenaltyinfo.org.

Dillehay, Ronald C., and M. Sandys. 1996. "Life under Wainwright v. Witt: Juror Dispositions and Death Qualification." *Law and Human Behavior* 20:147–64.

Drass, Kris A., Peter R. Gregware, and Michael Musheno. 1997. "Social, Cultural, and Temporal Dynamics of the AIDS Case Congregation: Early Years of the Epidemic." *Law and Society Review* 31:267–300.

D'Souza, Dinesh. 1995. *The End of Racism: Principles for a Multiracial Society.* New York: Free Press.

DuBois, W. E. B. 1981 [1896]. *The Souls of Black Folk.* New York: W. W. Norton.

Dumm, Thomas L. 1993. "The New Enclosures: Racism in the Normalized Community." In *Reading Rodney King: Reading Urban Uprising,* ed. R. Gooding-Williams. New York: Routledge.

Du Toit, Andries. 1993. "The Micro-Politics of Paternalism: The Discourses of Management and Resistance on South African Fruit and Wine Farms." *Journal of Southern African Studies* 19:314–36.

Elias, Robert. 1994. *Victims Still: The Political Manipulation of Crime Victims.* Newbury Park, CA: Sage.

Ewick, Patricia, and Susan S. Silbey. 1995. "Subversive Stories and Hegemonic Tales: Towards a Sociology of Narrative." *Law and Society Review* 29:197–226.

———. 1998. *The Commonplace of Law: Stories from Everyday Life.* Chicago: University of Chicago Press.

Feagin, Joe R., and Hernán Vera. 1995. *White Racism: The Basics*. New York: Routledge.

Fitzgerald, Robert, and Phoebe Ellsworth. 1984. "Due Process vs. Crime Control: Death Qualification and Jury Attitudes." *Law and Human Behavior* 8:31–55.

Fleury-Steiner, Benjamin. 2002. "Narratives of the Death Sentence: Toward a Theory of Legal Narrativity." *Law and Society Review* 36:549–76.

———. 2003. "Before or Against the Law? Citizens' Legal Beliefs and Experiences as Death Penalty Jurors." *Studies in Law, Politics, and Society* 27:115–37.

Foucault, Michel. 1979. *Discipline and Punish*. New York: Vintage.

Freedman, Alan David. 1978. "Legitimizing Racial Discrimination through Antidiscrimination Law: A Critical Review of Supreme Court Doctrine." *Minnesota Law Review* 62:1049–95.

Frye, Northrop. 1957. *Anatomy of Criticism*. Princeton: Princeton University Press.

Garfinkel, Harold. 1956. "Conditions of Successful Degradation Ceremonies." *American Journal of Sociology* 61:420–24.

Gilliam, Franklin D., Jr. 1999. "The 'Welfare Queen' Experiment." *Nieman Reports* 53 (2). http://www.nieman.harvard.edu/reports/992NRsummer99/Gilliam.html.

Goffman, Erving. 1963. *Stigma: Notes on the Management of Spoiled Identity*. New York: Simon and Schuster.

Goldberg-Hiller, Jonathan. 2002. *The Limits to Union: Same-Sex Marriage and the Politics of Civil Rights*. Ann Arbor: University of Michigan Press.

Gomez, Laura. 1998. "Constructing Latina/o Identities." *Chicano-Latino Law Review* 19:187–91.

Gramsci, Antonio. 1985. *Selections from Cultural Writings*. Cambridge: Harvard University Press.

Hagedorn, John M. 1998. *People and Folks: Gangs, Crime, and the Underclass in a Rustbelt City*. 2d ed. Chicago: Lakeview.

Haney, Craig. 1998. "Mitigation and the Study of Lives." In *America's Experiment with Capital Punishment*, ed. James R. Acker, Robert M. Bohm, and Charles S. Lanier. Durham, NC: Carolina Academic Press.

Haney, Craig, A. Hurtado, and L. Vega. 1994. "'Modern' Death Qualification: New Data on Its Biasing Effects." *Law and Human Behavior* 18:619–34.

Hitchens, C. 2000. *No One Left to Lie To: The Values of the Worst Family*. New York: Verso.

Hoch, Paul. 1979. *White Hero, Black Beast: Racism, Sexism, and the Mask of Masculinity*. London: Pluto.

Huang, W. S., and M. S. Vaughn. 1996. "Support and Confidence: Public

Attitudes toward Police." In *Americans View Crime and Justice: A National Public Opinion Survey*, ed. Timothy J. Flanagan and Dennis R. Longmire. Thousand Oaks, CA: Sage.

Hurwitz, Jon, and Mark Peffley. 1997. "Public Perceptions of Race and Crime: The Role of Racial Stereotypes." *American Journal of Political Science* 41:375–401.

———. 1998. *Perception and Prejudice: Race and Politics in the United States*. New Haven: Yale University Press.

Jackman, Mary R. 1996. *The Velvet Glove: Paternalism and Conflict in Gender, Class, and Race Relations*. Berkeley: University of California Press.

Jacobs, Ronald N. 2001. "The Problem with Tragic Narratives: Lesson from the Los Angeles Uprising." *Qualitative Sociology* 24:221–43.

Jamieson, Kathleen Hall. 1992. *Dirty Politics: Deception, Distraction, and Democracy*. New York: Oxford University Press.

Katz, Jack. 1988. *Seductions of Crime: Moral and Sensual Attractions in Doing Evil*. New York: Basic Books.

Kennedy, Randall. 1997. *Race, Crime, and the Law*. New York: Vintage.

Lawrence, Charles. 1987. "The Id, the Ego, and Equal Protection: Reckoning with Unconscious Racism." *Stanford Law Review* 39:317–61.

Lazarus, Edward P. 1998. *Closed Chambers: The First Eyewitness Account of the Epic Struggles Inside the Supreme Court*. New York: Times Books.

Lazarus-Black, Mindie, and Susan F. Hirsch, eds. 1994. *Contested States: Law, Hegemony, and Resistance*. New York: Routledge.

Lock, Shmuel. 1999. *Crime, Public Opinion, and Civil Liberties*. Westport, CT: Praeger.

Lott, Tommy L. 1999. *The Invention of Race: Black Culture and the Politics of Representation*. Malden, MA: Blackwell.

Loury, Glenn C. 2002. *The Anatomy of Racial Inequality*. Cambridge: Harvard University Press.

Luginbuhl, James, and Julie Howe. 1995. "Discretion in Capital Sentencing Instructions: Guided or Misguided?" *Indiana Law Journal* 70:1161–80.

Maguire, Kathleen, and Ann Pastore, eds. 1996. *Sourcebook of Criminal Justice Statistics*. Washington, DC: U.S. Bureau of Justice Statistics.

Mann, Coramae Richey, and Marjorie S. Zatz. 1998. *Images of Color, Images of Crime: Readings*. Los Angeles: Roxbury.

Massey, Douglas S. 1995. "Getting Away with Murder: Segregation and Violent Crime in Urban America." *University of Pennsylvania Law Review* 143:1203–32.

Mata, Alberto G., Jr. 1998. "Immigrant Bashing and Nativist Political Movements." In *Images of Color, Images of Crime*, ed. Coramae Richey Mann and Marjorie S. Zatz. Los Angeles: Roxbury.

Matsuda, Mari. 1989. "Public Response to Racist Speech: Considering the Victim's Story." *Michigan Law Review* 87:2320–72.

Mauer, Marc. 1999. *Race to Incarcerate*. New York: New Press.

McMahon, Jack. 1986. "Jury Selection with Jack McMahon." Transcript of DATV Productions videotype.

Mead, George H. 1918. "The Psychology of Punitive Justice." *American Journal of Sociology* 23:577–602.

Mirandé, Alfredo. 1987. *Gringo Justice*. Notre Dame, IN: University of Notre Dame Press.

Montoya, Margaret. 1998. "Religious Rituals and LatCrit Theorizing." *Chicano-Latino Law Review* 19:417–29.

Morris, Aldon D. 1986. *The Origins of the Civil Rights Movement: Black Communities Organizing for Change*. New York: Free Press.

Morrison, Toni, and Claudia Brodsky Lacour, eds. 1997. *Birth of a Nation 'Hood: Gaze, Script, and Spectacle in the O. J. Simpson Case*. New York: Pantheon.

Moynihan, Daniel Patrick. 1973. *The Politics of a Guaranteed Income: The Nixon Administration and the Family Assistance Plan*. New York: Random House.

Munger, Frank. 1998. "Immanence and Identity: Understanding Poverty through Law and Society Research." *Law and Society Review* 32:931–68.

Musto, David, 1973. *The American Disease: Origins of Narcotic Control*. New Haven: Yale University Press.

Nelson, Lars-Erik. 2000. "Color of Skin Can Be Fatal in Texas Courts." *New York Daily News,* June 7, p. 35.

Nielsen, Laura Beth. 2000. "Situating Legal Consciousness: Experiences and Attitudes of Ordinary Citizens about Law and Sexual Harassment." *Law and Society Review* 34:1055–90.

Oberweis, Trish, and Michael Musheno. 2001. *Knowing Rights: State Actors' Stories of Power, Identity, and Morality*. Burlington, VT: Ashgate.

Oliver, Melvin L., and Thomas M. Shapiro. 1995. *Black Wealth/White Wealth: A New Perspective on Racial Inequality*. New York: Routledge.

Olson, Susan M., and Christina Batjer. 1999. "Competing Narratives in a Judicial Retention Election: Feminism versus Judicial Independence." *Law and Society Review* 33:123–60.

Omi, Michael, and Howard Winant. 1994. *Racial Formation in the United States from the 1960s to the 1990s*. 2d ed. New York: Routledge.

Pyle, Jeffrey J. 1999. "Race, Equality, and the Rule of Law: Critical Race Theory's Attack on the Promises of Liberalism." *Boston College Law Review* 40:787–827.

Rabinowitz, Alan. 1990. *Social Change Philanthropy in America*. New York: Quorum.

Reinarman, Craig, and Harry G. Levine. 1997. *Crack in America: Demon Drugs and Social Justice*. Berkeley: University of California Press.

Riessman, Catherine Kohler. 1993. *Narrative Analysis*. Newbury Park, CA: Sage.

———. 1994. "Making Room for Diversity in Social Work Research." In *Qualitative Studies in Social Work Research,* ed. Catherine Kohler Riessman. Thousand Oaks, CA: Sage.

Robson, Ruthann. 1995. "To Market, to Market: Considering Class in the Context of Lesbian Legal Theories and Reforms." *Southern California Review of Law and Women's Studies* 5:173–84.

Rodriguez, Luis. 1994. "Throwaway Kids: Turning Youth Gangs Around." *The Nation,* November 21, 605–9.

Sanchez-Jankowski, Martin. 1992. *Islands in the Street: Gangs and American Urban Society*. Berkeley: University of California Press.

Sandys, Marla. 1995. "Cross-Overs—Capital Jurors Who Change Their Minds About the Punishment: A Litmus Test for Sentencing Guidelines." *Indiana Law Journal* 70:1183–221.

———. 1998. "Stacking the Deck for Guilt and Death: The Failure of Death Qualification to Ensure Impartiality." In *America's Experiment with Capital Punishment,* ed. James R. Acker, Robert M. Bohm, and Charles S. Lanier. Durham, NC: Carolina Academic Press.

Sarat, Austin. 1993. "Speaking of Death: Narratives of Violence in Capital Trials." *Law and Society Review* 27:19–58.

Sasson, Theodore. 1995. *Crime Talk: How Citizens Construct a Social Problem*. Hawthorne, NY: Aldine de Gruyter.

Scheck, Barry, Peter Neufeld, and Jim Dwyer. 2000. *Actual Innocence: Five Days to Execution and Other Dispatches from the Wrongly Convicted*. New York: Doubleday.

Scheingold, S. 1984. *The Politics of Law and Order: Street Crime and Public Policy*. New York: Longman.

Schutz, Alfred. 1970. *On Phenomenology and Social Relations: Selected Writings*. Ed. E. H. Wagner. Chicago: University of Chicago Press.

Scott, Marvin, and Stanford Lyman. 1968. "Accounts." *American Sociological Review* 33:46–62.

Silberstein, Sandra. 1988. "Ideology as Process: Gender Ideology in Courtship Narratives." In Alexandra Dundas Todd and Sue Fisher, eds., *Gender and Discourse: The Power of Talk*. Norwood, NJ: Ablex.

Steiker, Carol S., and Jordan M. Steiker. 1998. "Judicial Developments in Capital Punishment Law." In *America's Experiment with Capital Pun-*

ishment, ed. James R. Acker, Robert M. Bohm, and Charles S. Lanier. Durham, NC: Carolina Academic Press.

Steinberg, Stephen. 2001. *Turning Back: The Retreat from Racial Justice in American Thought and Policy.* Boston: Beacon.

Steiner, Benjamin D. 1999. "Race, Ideology, and Legal Action: The Case of Capital Sentencing Jurors." Ph.D. diss., Northeastern University.

———. 2001. "The Consciousness of Crime and Punishment: Reflections on Identity Politics and Law-Making in the War on Drugs." *Studies in Law, Politics, and Society* 23:185–212.

Steiner, Benjamin D., William J. Bowers, and Austin Sarat. 1999. "Folk Knowledge as Legal Action: Death Penalty Judgments and the Tenet of Early Release in a Culture of Mistrust and Punitiveness." *Law and Society Review* 33:461–506.

Sullivan, Mercer L. 1989. *"Getting Paid": Youth Crime and Work in the Inner City.* Ithaca: Cornell University Press.

Sunnafrank, Michael, and Norman E. Fontes. 1983. "General and Crime Related Racial Stereotypes and Influence on Juridic Decisions." *Cornell Journal of Social Relations* 17:1–15.

Sweeney, Laura T., and Craig Haney. 1992. "The Influence of Race on Sentencing: A Meta-Analytic Review of Experimental Studies." *Behavioral Sciences and the Law* 10:179–95.

Tabbarok, Alexander, and Eric Helland. 2000. "DNA Should Boost Support for the Death Penalty." *St. Louis Post-Dispatch,* September 26, p. B7.

Teitel, Ruti. 1997. "Human Rights Theory: Human Rights Genealogy." *Fordham Law Review* 66:301–17.

Thompson, William C. 1989. "Death Qualification after *Wainwright v. Witt* and *Lockhart v. McCree.*" *Law and Human Behavior* 13:185–207.

Tonry, Michael. 1997. *Malign Neglect: Race, Crime, and Punishment in America.* New York: Oxford University Press.

Van den Haag, Ernest. 1975. *Punishing Criminals: Concerning a Very Old and Painful Question.* New York: Basic Books.

van Dijk, Teun A. 1993. "Stories and Racism." In *Narrative and Social Control: Critical Perspectives,* ed. Dennis K. Mumby. Thousand Oaks, CA: Sage.

Vigil, James Diego. 1988. *Barrio Gangs: Street Life and Identity in Southern California.* Austin: University of Texas Press.

Walker, Samuel, Cassia Spohn, and Miriam DeLone. 2000. *The Color of Justice: Race, Ethnicity, and Crime in America.* Belmont, CA: Wadsworth.

Weisberg, Robert. 1983. "Deregulating Death." *Supreme Court Review* 1983:305–95.

West, Candace, and Don H. Zimmerman. 1987. "Doing Gender." *Gender and Society* 1:125–51.

Wildman, Stephanie M. 1996. *Privilege Revealed: How Invisible Preference Undermines America.* New York: New York University Press.

Williams, Terence T. 1989. *The Cocaine Kids: The Inside Story of a Teenage Drug Ring.* Reading, MA: Addison-Wesley.

Wilmore, G. S. 1998. *Black Religion and Black Radicalism: An Interpretation of the Religious History of African Americans.* Chicago: Orbis.

Wilson, W. J. 1987. *The Truly Disadvantaged: The Inner City, the Underclass, and Public Policy.* Chicago: University of Chicago Press.

———. 1997. *When Work Disappears: The World of the New Urban Poor.* New York: Knopf.

Wolfe, Christopher. 1991. *Judicial Activism: Bulwark of Freedom or Precarious Security?* London: Thomson.

Wright, Richard. 1940. *Native Son.* New York: Harper and Brothers.

Author Index

Subject Index

Capital defendants
  childhood trauma, 106, 112
  crime and the life course, 116
  gangs, 116–17
  multiple risk factors, 170n. 5
  predictable harm, 170n. 5
Capital jurors
  attitudes and beliefs, 84, 142–51,
    159, 173n. 13, 174n. 16, 175n. 2,
    180n. 2, 181n. 5
  death predisposition, 25, 26, 91,
    176n. 1 (chap. 5)
  death qualification, 6, 24–26, 28,
    29, 59–60, 66, 78, 87, 130, 131,
    140–41, 142, 144, 148, 151,
    170n. 6, 180n. 2
  decision making, 8, 10, 20, 24, 25,
    28, 30, 33–34, 35, 38, 44, 56, 79,
    95, 106, 173n. 13, 180n. 1
    (app. B)
  homophobia, 58
  life holdouts, 107–25
  racial stereotypes, 25, 57, 98, 101,
    173n. 13
  resisters, 103–29
Capital Jury Project
  interview strategy, 30–31
  sample characteristics, 175n. 4
  sampling design, 31, 175n. 4
Crystal methamphetamine,
  103–5

Death penalty
  death qualification, 6, 24–26, 28,
    29, 59–60, 66, 78, 87, 130, 131,

140–41, 142, 144, 148, 151,
    170n. 6, 180n. 2
  devaluing of victim status, 57–58
  DNA as "silver bullet," 179n. 3
  erroneous death sentences, 16,
    179n. 3
  privileging one life over another,
    134–35
  "reform," 136, 179n. 3
Decision making
  challenges of resisting the major-
    ity, 140–41
  constituting the holdout as
    "unstable," 125
  deceitful manipulation, 125
  degradation ritual, 127–28
  educating resisters, 119–20, 133
  gender, 57–58
  group dynamics, 122, 127
  isolation, 74–75
  paternalism, 42, 54–56, 93, 96–97,
    178n. 3
Deindustrialization, 178n. 2
  barrio poor, 117

Factor analysis, 180n. 3, 181n. 4

Gay rights, legal backlash against,
  176n. 2

Identity
  "doing gender," 178nn. 4, 5
  insider, 9, 72, 130–33, 137–42,
    175n. 3, 178n. 3, 180n. 1 (app.
    A), 182n. 7

197

Race
  black jurors and civil rights
    activism, 67
  black oppression, 169n. 3
  crime and punishment attitudes,
    26, 27
  criminal justice policies, 17
  critical race theory, 16–17,
    171n. 7
  death sentencing outcomes, 3, 12,
    13, 23, 66, 177n. 1
  "double consciousness," 71
  ideology, 171n. 7
  incarceration, 17
  Lat crit (Latino/a critical) theory,
    171n. 7
  limits of traditional liberal views,
    17
  masculinity, 15, 43
  multiculturalism, 133
  patterns of crime, 176n. 3
  "perpetrator perspective," 17
  religiosity, 160
  residential segregation, 2, 67,
    178n. 1
  reverse discrimination, 17
  Rodney King spectacle, 177n. 3
  weakening of civil rights laws,
    170n. 2
  wealth inequality, 138–39
  whiteness, 54, 177n. 3
  white privilege, 68–70, 176n. 3

South Africa, abolition of death
    penalty, 134–35
Supreme Court
  decline of liberal dissent, 23–24
  Justice Brennan's fears of contin-
    ued racial discrimination, 129
  Justice Scalia's "*McCleskey*
    memo," 172n. 11
  Lockhart decision, 26
  McCleskey decision, 8, 11–14, 18,
    23, 129, 170n. 1, 172n. 11
  punishment at all costs, 23,
    172n. 11